the BREAKTHROUGH FACTOR

FROM SUCCESS TO SIGNIFICANCE

HENRY MARSH

Manufactured in the United States of America

10 9 8 7 6 5 4 3 2 1

Library of Congress Cataloging-in-Publication Data

Marsh, Henry (Henry D.).
The breakthrough factor: from success to significance / Henry Marsh.
p. cm.
1. Success—Psychological aspects. 2. Values. I. Title.
BF637.S8M288   2013   97-12478   CIP
158.1—dc21
ISBN: 978-0-9888401-0-2

Grateful acknowledgment is made to Russell & Volkening as agents for the autor for permission to reprint material excerpted from *The X Factor* by George Plimpton. Copyright © 1995 by George Plimpton.

This book is dedicated to James, Danielle, Andrew, Lauren, Casey, and Zander, with the hope that the concepts presented herein will help you create a life of values for your success and happiness.

TABLE OF CONTENTS

CHAPTER SIX 89
DON'T SACRIFICE WHAT YOU WANT
MOST FOR WHAT YOU WANT NOW

CHAPTER SEVEN 103
EXERCISE ONLY ON THE DAYS YOU EAT

INTRODUCTION

THE PRINCIPLE MADE ME DO IT!

There is an incredible power within each of us that is the way to achieving our personal best. It is the power of principles.

I t's the principle of the thing!" is a phrase that has been around our culture as long as anyone can remember. When all other reasons have been exhausted, it's the one given for continuing on. Beyond money, beyond power, beyond glory, even beyond winning, things are done simply "on principle."

Our principles make us do it.

This book is about principles. It's about what they are, how we get them, why we all have them, and what we use them for.

Most of all, it's about power. The incredible power of principles. A power so pervasive, so all encompassing, that there isn't anything any of us do that can't be traced back to its source. In short, our behavior is a reflection of the principles we choose to live by.

Some of us recognize and understand this power and use it for all it's worth. Others use it from time to time, but don't realize what it is they're using. And too often, many of us leave this source of power largely untapped in our lives, as if we had Michael Jordan on the team and kept him on the end of the bench.

This is not a book about morals. You'll find nothing here that preaches what values you ought to have; what you should believe. The focus is on recognizing that the beliefs we individually choose to live by are directly responsible for whatever quality of life we enjoy. There's just no getting around that. That's life! The key to enjoying peace, success, fulfillment, and contentment is putting in place those beliefs that will best produce those kinds of satisfying results. That's the challenge to each of us: to find out what beliefs allow us to realize our personal bests.

I use the phrase "personal best" because for thirteen years I competed in international athletics, and those were words I learned to greatly respect. I participated as a middle-distance runner on four United States Olympic teams. From 1976 through 1988, I was the top American in the 3,000-meter steeplechase, setting four American records and being ranked number one in the world three times. I continuously held the American record for 26 years (1980–2006) and was inducted into the U.S.A. Track and Field Hall of Fame.

Those American records were built on an athletic career of personal bests. Every year I attempted to improve my personal best. That was my measuring stick. Was I running faster than ever before? And each year as I set new personal bests I felt great personal fulfillment. Early in my career, when I ran my fastest time, it was simply my own personal best—my own record. Later, when four of my personal bests were also American records, or American bests, they took on an added measure of notoriety. But those earlier "individual" personal bests brought the same satisfaction as the American personal bests that came later.

Personally, I can tell you that my entire experience as an athlete was an extremely satisfying "run," and I'm convinced it was because I had principles that allowed me to concentrate on striving for my own personal best rather than worrying about someone else's personal best. Because of those inward-directed principles, I was not only able to compete for as long as I did, but I was able to thoroughly enjoy the experience.

Just as I sought to achieve personal bests athletically, we can seek to achieve personal bests in all areas of our lives. In this book, we'll learn how. Better yet, we can achieve personal bests well after our physiological peak or age—which limits us athletically. We can have greater fulfillment every day we live upon the earth.

As a runner, I happened to plug into the power of principles without consciously realizing what I was doing—and not only did that save my career in the beginning, it saved me from experiencing a lot of unnecessary grief during those times when things didn't go my way. Looking back, all I can say is thank goodness my focus was on "personal best" and not "gold medal."

I understand now why I didn't quit, and why others either wanted to or did. I understand now why I was able to avoid the angst that can so often be an integral part of a career as competitive as international track and field. I understand now why I was able to deal with what the world would term "devastating setbacks." It was because I had my own finish line. I could "win" when others only saw losing. I had a different principle.

I've seen this same principle at work in my experiences with many MonaVie distributors. Those distributors who set a goal of becoming phenomenally wealthy are often—but not always—frustrated in the results. On the other hand, those distributors whose life and work are governed by the principle of helping others achieve more meaning in their lives are inevitably successful. They're also more often than not financially successful as well.

So I am "Exhibit A" in the pages that follow. I use myself as a living example of one who has experienced the power of beliefs in achieving one's personal best. It happened to me as a runner, and it happened to me again as an attorney. I graduated from law school, passed the bar exam, and began to practice law, all set to climb the legal ladder of fulfillment and success. But I discovered I was not cut out to spend my days in a law library, and I made a career change just when I was ready to cash in on all my years of preparation and training. The beliefs that pushed me to achieve my personal best also pushed me to be one of the founders of MonaVie—an international company built not only on the personal bests of its founders, but on the personal bests of literally thousands of independent distributors. In the pages that follow, I detail the dynamics that caused my career change as an attorney and the beliefs that led me to play a part in the creation of MonaVie because they further help illustrate, and endorse, the power of applying beliefs that work for your own purposes. Not for anyone else's; for your own.

I've been a few places and done a few things, and I've made some big principle-driven changes along the way that have made all the difference—and if it's true that you can't effectively sell something unless you believe in it wholeheartedly yourself, in the chapters to come you'll see I've taken care of that requirement.

Like many of us, I happened quite by chance upon the power of principle-driven behavior. But it doesn't need to happen that way. It is possible to become consciously aware of our beliefs and take care that they drive the kind of behavior that will produce the quality of life we're seeking. It's possible to realize going in that our beliefs tell us what to do! Once we understand that, we can start putting beliefs in place that will not let us be satisfied with mere success, but will inspire us to breakthrough and push beyond success to significance. In other words, we can start putting beliefs in place to achieve our personal best.

Forks in the Road

A few years ago I saw a bumper sticker that read: GUNS DON'T KILL PEOPLE, PEOPLE KILL PEOPLE. I thought the point was well made. A gun is powerless until somebody decides to use it. A gun has no mind of its own; it can't make decisions. It is simply the extension of the behavior of the person using it; a whim at the beck and call of whoever's finger is on the trigger.

To illustrate the point, here are two names for you: Mahatma Gandhi and Adolf Hitler.

In many significant ways, these men were alike. By all accounts, they each had superior intelligence, excellent speaking skills, incredible powers of persuasion, and the ability to inspire others to follow them and embrace their causes. They were goal setters. They had charisma. In short, they each had the qualities of leadership.

But despite their similarities, they couldn't have behaved much more differently.

Hitler's politics were fueled by beliefs of superiority. He believed in the supremacy of the Aryan race and acted accordingly. Armed with this belief, he was able to order the execution of millions of people and invade and dominate millions more. Gandhi, on the other hand, acted according to an entirely different set of beliefs, based on the sanctity of all human life. Because the Indian leader's aims were to improve the quality of life for his people, his behavior was on the other end of the spectrum from Hitler's. Whereas Hitler embraced violence, Gandhi eschewed it. One waged war. One waged peace.

Both behaved according to their personal truths—and that made all the difference.

It's There, Might As Well Use It

We all behave according to beliefs. We can't help it. We can't avoid it. There's no getting around it. It's a universal thing. It's like eating and sleeping. If we're alive, we do it. Whether we do it consciously or subconsciously, we all do it.

The simple act of breathing can actually help illustrate this distinction between conscious and subconscious action. Most of us go through our days breathing every few seconds and hardly give it a conscious thought. But those who understand the value of breathing do give it a conscious thought. Proper diaphragm breathing—inhaling deep into the diaphragm, or stomach, area to ensure a full exchange of oxygen and carbon dioxide—allows for better circulation, sharper instincts, and optimum coordination. Athletes learn how to breathe. So do dancers and performers and those who practice yoga and other forms of meditation. Breathing, at its best, let's us fall asleep, calms us down, makes us healthier, and helps us make free throws and perform a virtuoso *Swan Lake*. Breathing is, in fact, a tremendous power, whether we realize it or not. Some people use it as a power quite naturally. But most don't. Most have to either work at it, or they end up not getting the most out of something valuable that's completely available to them.

It's the same with principle-driven behavior. We are all driven by our beliefs, every last one of us. Our behavior is unavoidably a mirror image of our beliefs, but most of us are unaware of the power inherent in that natural resource. We use it unconsciously. We use it without even knowing it. We have the power of a Ferrari under the hood, and we barely touch the gas pedal.

To really tap into this power source—and, as a result, achieve our personal best—we need to understand it, understand that we have it, and understand what to do with it. Time and again I have seen the importance of getting in touch with beliefs and the behavior that they drive. When that behavior delivers unsatisfactory results, it only makes sense that it ought to be changed, for the most basic of reasons: Who doesn't want to have satisfactory results in their lives? The only way to effectively change behavior is by changing the belief that's prompting it.

Through my experiences as a competitive athlete and my professional experiences both as an attorney and with MonaVie, I have become an avid student and ardent proponent of seeking to achieve one's personal best through belief-driven behavior. It has not only become my life's work, but it's helped me to understand just how much more effective and valuable it is when belief-driven behavior is understood. It's helped me realize that some of the belief changes I personally went through earlier in my life could have occurred much earlier—if I had known then what I know now.

I have seen countless people, many of whose stories are included in this book, who have benefited greatly by consciously seeking to better their lives through principle-driven behavior. The quality of their lives improved by first identifying their current beliefs, then recognizing the need to change the beliefs that were driving destructive behavior, and, finally, doing what was necessary to change them.

As with anything worthwhile, it's not always easy. Once in place, a belief—whether it's good or bad for us—can be mighty stubborn and difficult to budge. There are physiological factors at work, as well as psychological ones, that make us as loath to give up a belief-in-place as we would a thousand-dollar bill.

Unwitting Accomplices

We'll see in the following pages that too often we're unwitting accomplices in unproductive plots that undermine the quality of our own lives—plots that are usually entirely self-determined! We'll see that many of our beliefs were acquired in our youth before we even realized what we were acquiring—and how, as a result, we can easily get caught up in unrelenting cycles of negative behavior that perpetuate the same unsatisfactory results.

We'll see the danger in short-term, diversionary remedies; modern day "fixes" that don't get to the core of our problems, that don't really effect change, but only mask the pain—pain that is a direct result of not realizing our needs. We'll see how these short-term cures, which do nothing about changing our beliefs, can turn into addictions that are capable of further entrenching us in unwanted and unproductive patterns: addictions that range from drug dependence (legal and illegal) to oversleeping to shopping; addictions that contribute to modern-day diseases such as most forms of hypertension, numerous forms of depression, and many other stress-related problems so prevalent in our society. We'll see how just coping with these diseases can occupy an enormous amount of time, energy, and expense and prevent us from building the kind of lives we really want by getting to the root of our behavior: our beliefs.

We'll explore the importance of having positive "self-talks" to maintain our newfound powers, and the importance of practicing preventive maintenance. We'll talk about the importance of being well rounded and of getting in touch with what we want most—as opposed to what we want now! We'll examine the basic needs we all share and the way they unavoidably affect our satisfaction with life. We'll probe constructive ways to get beyond the static of daily life and understand what our beliefs really are, and how to begin to achieve our personal best by learning how to come up with our own theoretical new beliefs.

We'll explore control—not the need for it, but the need to understand it—to know what we can control and what we can't, and to act accordingly. There are no cure-alls to avoid hardships. Obstacles are a given. Life is not always fair, and even having empowering beliefs in place won't change that. But having empowering beliefs in place puts life's obstacles in a perspective that makes them manageable. We can flow around them instead of constantly bumping into them head-on.

An Owner's Manual

This book is about quality of life: an owner's manual on how to achieve our personal best in life, both personally and professionally, through principle-driven behavior. When we know what's driving us, we're in a position to see if it will take us where we want to go. There are tips here to help us know—and, once we know, understand—how to go about realizing our potential.

Principle-driven behavior is driven from within. The purpose of this book isn't to identify beliefs that are right or wrong. Instead, we'll identify beliefs that are either empowering or hindering, depending on the behavior they drive and the needs that are satisfied as a result.

It is within the reach of each of us, independently, to establish beliefs that empower us, beliefs that in turn will drive behavior that will produce satisfying results in our individual lives. What do we really want? That's the universal question. Do we want to be a better salesman, a better husband or wife, a better parent, a better golfer or bowler, a better CEO, a better public speaker, a better distributor, a better business builder? Do we want to have better health, better security, a better feeling about ourselves?

I don't care what it is, we can achieve it by finding the empowering belief. We can search for our empowering beliefs in a wide variety of places, both from within and without. People whose results we admire and don't admire—whether we know them personally or not, from all walks of life, are fair game: from leaders of commerce and politics, from sports figures to coworkers, from uplines to sidelines, from our friends and neighbors to members of our own family. If we observe their behavior and find we would like to emulate it, then our task becomes a simple one of understanding the belief that drives that behavior and adopting it as one of our own. The opposite holds, too. Once we've identified them, we're also in a position to avoid the beliefs of those whose behavior we find harmful and unfulfilling.

The key is finding those beliefs, not merely observing behavior as is so often our natural tendency. Imitating may be the most sincere form of flattery, but it isn't the best way to achieve our personal best. When I was a teenager, I remember going to the movies and watching Robert Redford in *Jeremiah Johnson*, a movie about a mountain man. The lead character had a big impact on me. I liked his toughness and his ability to handle difficult situations. I left the theater deciding I would be like Jeremiah Johnson, and for a few days I acted like him: not saying much, holding a kind of steely stare—an impenetrable mountain man. But the impersonation, such as it was, soon passed. I returned to being me. In order to effectively behave like Jeremiah Johnson, I would have needed to get in touch with the beliefs that drove him. Since I wasn't willing to chuck everything I had, buy a mule, and head into the wilderness, I didn't have much of a chance to truly understand what those beliefs might have been. I could have done that. If it had been important enough to me, if I had felt it would have greatly enhanced my quality of life, I could have headed for the hills.

True Freedom

Beyond "borrowing" the beliefs we see and admire in others, when we objectively identify our own beliefs we buy ourselves real freedom—true freedom that allows us to be in charge of ourselves; to not feel like we have to copy others or be slaves to conformity.

When we know that we have the authority to alter those beliefs that bring us undue stress, unhappiness, pain, and sadness, and that lower our quality of life—even if they might seem to work for others—we're in a position to truly chart our own course. We have ownership over ourselves.

In my days as a steeplechase runner, there was a time when I made a significant change in my training philosophy and technique, a change I was able to make only because of a new outlook I formed about my training principles. It had to do with my hurdling style. I had always gone off the same foot when jumping over a hurdle, just like everyone else. But I decided I wouldn't do that anymore. I decided I'd practice being able to jump off either foot because I felt that would work better for me. I could clear the hurdles wrong-footed. It was unorthodox. Nobody coached it that way at the time. Few ran that way. But I said, "So what?" and tried it anyway. The only reason I was able to do that was because I'd decided not to look at how others did it anymore. I'd adopted a new belief. It was that decision that freed me up to go ahead and be unconventional. And it did help. Without that change, and some others I'll talk about in detail later, I don't believe I'd have made my first Olympic team, let alone the other three. In short, I gave myself the freedom to chart my own course and achieve the best that was in me.

Feelings of Control

The power I stumbled onto and then tapped into that allowed me to dramatically improve was the very power this book is about: the power of achieving personal best through principle-driven behavior. I know firsthand that this power is capable of bringing about truly dramatic results. I know it can result in feelings of personal control, self-management, contentment, and inner peace. Altering our beliefs—the way we look at life—really can facilitate significant change in meaning in our lives.

Whether we realize it or not, beliefs fuel us. They are what generate our actions or our inactions. They can propel us, thrust us, urge us, catapult us, move us—choose your verb—and, conversely, they can inhibit us, freeze us, delay us, and hold us back.

In *Webster's New World Dictionary,* a principle is defined as "the ultimate source, origin, or cause of something," and "a fundamental truth, law, doctrine, or motivating force, upon which others are based." In this book we will use Webster's definition of "principle" to see how our "personal truths" interact with "fundamental truths" or principles to forcefully motivate each of us. Since we form our personal truths based on what we believe will meet our needs, we will use the term "belief" interchangeably with "personal truth."

Timeless and Universal

It thrills me to realize that what first worked for me in college wasn't a quirk or a fluke, but a power that is both timeless and universal: the power of achieving your personal best through principle-driven behavior. It's the same power that drove Benjamin Franklin to all his accomplishments more than two hundred years ago (he understood it). It's the same power that can drive us all to the lives we'd like to have.

In the following pages, we'll walk through the whys, the wherefores, and the how-to's of meaningful change. Together, we will uncover what truly motivates us, what drives us in our lives. We'll look at those things that produce unhappiness in our lives, as well as happiness, and realize just how much control we have over both areas.

In the book's first half we will look at a very powerful behavior model which I call the Belief Paradigm. This paradigm enables us to better see what drives us in our lives, what motivates us, and why we behave the way we do. As a visual tool, this model can help us see just how our beliefs, behavior, results, and needs are all interrelated. It helps us visualize how those things we learned in our early formative years are in fact powerfully driving us yet today. We'll realize that only by accurately identifying our true beliefs can we put ourselves in a position to change those beliefs that we discover do not empower us to achieve our life's goals; and by changing those beliefs, we'll drive the behavior that will fulfill our potential.

We'll also look at the physical, mental, and emotional challenges that we all encounter, and we'll look at the importance of analyzing our actions "over time."

In the book's second half we'll look at specific steps we can take to achieve our personal best through principle-driven behavior. We'll look at things we can do to build ourselves up. We'll look at ways we can take control of those events that cause us anxiety and contribute to feelings of little or no control.

Most important, we'll look at time-proven ways to effectively form new empowering beliefs and eliminate those hindering beliefs that produce unproductive behavior, undesirable results, and feelings of despair in our lives. We'll look at the need to focus on what works for us—the need to focus on what will produce lives of contentment and inner peace. We'll learn how to take the theory outlined in the following pages and apply it in our lives so the theory becomes reality.

As I have traveled back and forth in my work, crisscrossing the globe, I have had a ringside seat, as it were, from which to observe people making dramatic improvements in their lives through principle-driven behavior. It's a thrilling sight. I'd like you to see those sights through my eyes.

You'll see I'm a big fan of achieving personal best through principle-driven behavior. I'm a recipient of the positive benefits myself, and I've seen many others benefit as well. This power we're about to explore has helped me appreciate the ability we all have to control our own lives, to become our best. It's a power that's helped me avoid a lot of negativity and has greatly enhanced my quality of life. For one thing, I know it helped me run faster. I know it can help you run faster, too.

— Henry Marsh

CHAPTER ONE

PRINCIPLE-DRIVEN BEHAVIOR
THE NEED-BELIEF-BEHAVIOR CONNECTION

An overview of the Belief Paradigm, which diagrams the dynamics of human behavior and explains why we, and those around us, behave the way we do.

We all have them. We all try to satisfy them. They compel us, they prod us, they motivate us, they propel us, they steer us, they captivate us.

Twenty-four hours a day.

Every day.

Needs.

Needs are something the entire human family has in common. No matter where we live, how much we own, what language we speak, or the color of our skin, we're alike in that we all have needs: needs that drive our behavior and provide the basis and impetus for everything we do. It is the reality of needs that causes us to develop our personal truths in the first place.

Although as individuals we can be vastly different, our basic needs as human beings are nonetheless identical. They're the same for a billionaire on the Gold Coast of Long Island as they are for a beggar on the streets of Calcutta. There is no difference.

Many of us aren't even consciously aware of exactly what these needs are. Sometimes it's not until we look backward that they come into clear focus.

In a survey conducted by Dr. Gerald Bell of the University of North Carolina, four thousand retired executives were asked this question: If you could live your life over, what would you do differently? Across the board their answers reflected a desire to take better ownership of their lives. In essence they responded that life isn't practice. Every day is the Super Bowl. It's the real thing.

These executives, all of them very successful by material standards, talked of taking better care of their health (not throwing away their health as if it were trash), spending more time with their families, spending more time on personal development or having more fun, and paying more attention to spiritual development and community service. Give them another turn and they displayed an overwhelming desire to take care of those things that, after seventy-plus years, they viewed as their most cherished and important values.

They were articulating their needs—and not what they may have once thought were their needs, but the ones they now knew were their needs.

The Four Basic Needs

Besides offering a perspective with the clarity of twenty-twenty hindsight, Dr. Bell's survey reaffirmed that as humans we are driven by four basic needs—needs that make up the Belief Paradigm's Needs Quadrants. (See illustration on following page.) After careful examination, the desires of the retired executives, as for all of us, could clearly be assigned to one of these four basic need categories:

- Live
- Love
- Enjoy
- Self-esteem

Think of the things that are most important in your life—those things you desire most—and you'll find it's possible to fit all of them into one or all of the above categories: to live, to love, to enjoy, and to have a feeling of self-esteem. These are the needs that drive our lives, all of our lives. Fulfilling them, or trying to, is what causes us to do the things we do. When we're successful at meeting these needs, life is satisfying; it's great to be alive; we have hope, enthusiasm, zest; we look forward to tomorrow.

When we're not successful—and it's amazing how out of sync we can get when even one of the four basic needs isn't taken care of—life is often just the opposite. It can be drudgery just to get out of bed and start the day.

One by one, let's look at our four common needs and define them further.

The first of these needs, the need to live, is basic physical survival. To stay alive is the most primal of all the needs and the most enduring. It's the need to have food and shelter and protection from the elements so we don't die. It could also be described as the survival need.

The common expression, "No one wants to die," is probably better said in its more positive form: "Everyone wants to live." As has been manifest over and over again throughout history, the desire to live is so strong that we will go to enormous lengths and spend great amounts of energy when our survival need is threatened. In primitive times, the need to live was easily identified and revealed in daily efforts such as finding food, shelter, and protection. In modern times, the need to live is revealed in such ways as our concern for our finances, our health, our clothes, and our homes. We feel a need to be comfortable and secure, to avoid as much as possible those dangers that threaten our ability simply to live. It is the same need that pushes us to find better opportunities and to improve upon our current situations. We seek out better jobs or new careers, as well as ways to supplement our income, all in the hope of achieving more meaning in our lives.

The second need, the love need, is the desire we all have for intimate relationships. This is the need to have someone to watch a sunset or go to the opera with. In general, it's a social need. It's the need to share life with another. It's the need to love and be loved. We all have a need to belong, whether it's in our families, our work groups, our social clubs, or wherever. The love need is manifested in the time and energy we spend searching for, developing, and maintaining relationships with others. Often this need is met through building strong and close-knit downlines and teams.

The third need, the need to enjoy, is the spice of life need. This is the desire for the things that make our lives fun and interesting. It's what we get excited and enthused about, what we choose to do in our spare time, what we find rewarding and fulfilling—in short, all those things we enjoy doing. We all have a strong need to be able to do different things and have plenty of options. We don't like to wear the same clothes every day, or eat the same lunch. We like variety. Sameness bores us. Even if we don't realize it, we go to great lengths to satisfy this need for variety. It's a major factor in our job selection. It is why people bungee jump, or sky dive, or collect stamps, or any of thousands of other things that bring diversity to life.

The fourth need, the self-esteem need, is the one I think is the most compelling for us today. Our self-esteem need is what gives meaning to our lives. It is who we are in the world we live in. This need encompasses religious convictions. It is also our need for self-esteem, for a feeling of acceptance, for a positive self-image. It's the way we look at ourselves and think of ourselves, and the way we perceive that others look and think of us. We need to feel like we matter or we'll have no real incentive to live. This, I think, is especially true in our modern world, when we typically find ourselves with more discretionary time for social interchange. As with all of the needs, we will go to great lengths to satisfy our self-esteem need. It has a tremendous influence on the cars we drive, the homes we live in, the jobs we choose, the clubs we join, the clothes we wear, and so on. Not feeling important can cause us to question the reason for living. According to the National Institute of Health, in 2007 suicide was the tenth leading cause of death, but among teenagers that number jumped to the third leading cause of death. Why? Primarily, because their self-esteem need was not being met.

These, then, are our needs categories. We all have them, and on a regular, if not daily, basis we spend our lives attempting to satisfy these four basic needs. Think about it. They are what drive us and motivate us in everything we do. A balanced life maintains all four needs with a measure of equality, creating a well-rounded and generally smooth ride through life. An unbalanced life may overcompensate for one or two of the basic needs and neglect the others, or neglect all of them. The result is a life that is not fully round. In a worst-case scenario, unproductive, uninspired lives produce existences that are flat and don't roll at all, with none of the needs being satisfied. In a best-case scenario, all four needs areas are satisfied, and our lives, as a result, are productive, inspiring, and fulfilling.

Every day, meeting our needs, or trying to, is what we're all about. It stands to reason that all four needs require regular maintenance to be satisfied. They all require attention. When they're not satisfied, they'll cry out in any number of ways to get our attention. Sometimes we choose to listen. Sometimes we don't.

The Belief Paradigm

If we agree that meeting those various needs to our own satisfaction is what will bring us the peace and contentment we want, it's important to understand the paths we take, consciously or subconsciously, in our effort to satisfy those needs.

This is where the Belief Paradigm comes in. The connection between our needs, beliefs, and behavior isn't complicated, and it doesn't offer any guarantees to a happy life. What it does offer is a kind of life blueprint that can help us see if our needs are being met, and if not, what ought to be altered so they can be met. The Belief Paradigm helps us see our own reality. By doing so, we can then better assess our beliefs and the behavior they drive. So, let's go through the connection step by step.

The Belief Lens

After beginning with your needs, the Belief Paradigm moves to what is called the Belief Lens. (See illustration on following page.) Unlike the necessities that are common to all of us, everyone has his or her own Belief Lens. We're all issued our own lens when we're born. It's what each of us looks through to see the world. Each Belief Lens is going to be unique—a one of a kind—and we look through it every moment of every day, all day long. Everything that happens, everything we experience, everything we see is viewed through our lens. As it comes through the lens, we interpret it based on the beliefs we've established and built through our life experiences. Every new experience we have, we add another belief on our Belief Lens and further affect its composition.

These beliefs become the "why" behind our behavior; they provide the power that drives what we do and how we act. As we attempt to meet our needs, we form beliefs. Then, based on our view, we establish our own personal beliefs. We can only see the world as we've experienced it, so it follows that it's our life's experiences that make up our frame of reference, our reality, our truth. And we write that truth in the form of beliefs on our Belief Lens.

A study done by a major stock brokerage company helps to illustrate how our beliefs affect our behavior, and ultimately our outcomes. The study compared very successful brokers with their less successful counterparts. The interesting result of the study wasn't that the successful brokers necessarily worked harder than the rest, but, rather, that their belief of what they were doing was different. The less successful brokers saw their employment as a means to make a lot of money—their Belief Lens interpreted their employment as a way to satisfy their need for a large income. The successful brokers saw instead an opportunity to help other people. Through their lens, they viewed their work as a form of service, and approached every opportunity with excitement and sincerity. Because of their belief, these successful brokers were able to help more people and, ultimately, were more successful.

This same principle holds true in MonaVie. Those distributors focused on making another dollar are often frustrated with their lack of success. Meanwhile, those distributors who focus on the success of others find that they are simultaneously building their own success.

Belief Lenses and the beliefs on them are why we have different political parties, so many different religions, so many different biases and opinions, so many different viewpoints. We all have different experiences, so we all have different Belief Lenses. Think of it in terms of a pair of glasses. We see the world based on what kind of prescription is on our glasses, and it's our beliefs that create our prescriptions. Since we all have different sets of beliefs, like fingerprints, we're all going to have different prescriptions.

We're All Different

It's important to remember that it's our different experiences that create our different prescriptions. If we're raised in Somalia, for instance, we'll see the world a lot differently than if we're raised in the United States. If we're raised Catholic, we'll see the world a lot differently than if we're raised Jewish. If we're raised in an African-American community, we'll see the world a lot differently than if we're raised in a white community. And if we're raised in an integrated community, it would also cause us to see the world differently.

Multi-level marketing is a perfect example of how prescriptions vary. For some people, multi-level marketing—also called relationship or network marketing—has a very negative stigma attached to it. They've heard the horror stories of "snake-oil" products or pyramid schemes. They may even have been pressured into joining a multi-level marketing opportunity, or they know someone who was, and it didn't turn out well. Meanwhile, there are others who are a part of a multi-level marketing opportunity and have enjoyed phenomenal success. They have changed their own lives for the better and have played a major role in helping others to do the same. Put yourself in the shoes of either group—what would be your prescription when it comes to multi-level marketing? When the beliefs on your lens change, your opinion of multi-level marketing—or anything, for that matter—will also change. We define how we see the world based on the beliefs etched into our Belief Lens.

Not long after the fall of the Soviet Bloc, I found myself in Eastern Europe traveling through several of the countries that had emerged from Soviet communism and were now entering their free eras. In talking with the people in the midst of this transformation, I inquired as to their feelings on this change.

Being a true red-white-and-blue, apple-pie-eating, flag-saluting American, I fully anticipated a reply that went something like this: "Freedom is wonderful. All our lives we dreamed of this day. Our prayers have been answered. Now we can travel as we please, do as we want, with no restrictions from the state. We can choose our job, we can choose where we want to live, we can vote for whomever we wish, we can read what we want, we can worship as we please, and we don't have to stand in any more lines unless we want to."

I'd based my expectations in large part on personal experiences I'd had with Iron Curtain athletes who expressed a desire to defect. I particularly remember a Hungarian athlete at a meet in West Germany clutching a miniature Statue of Liberty as if to say, "I want to defect."

What I expected, however, wasn't what I got.

I was surprised at the wariness with which most people were "embracing" their newfound freedom. Many of the older people longed for the "good old days" when they were told where to work, where to shop, where to live, where they could and could not go, and what to eat. For all of their lives they had lived under a certain system; a system that, right or wrong, had been their lives. Embracing a new system was going to take a while. I heard several people say, "Freedom is overrated."

I was taken aback, of course. From my upbringing and my experience, I regarded freedom as more important than anything else. "Give me freedom or give me death." That was my prescription. I was surprised when I ran into people who had a prescription that in many ways was exactly the opposite.

Word Games

I've found that playing a word association game can help illustrate this point about different prescriptions on our Belief Lens. I'm going to give you a word and you blurt out whatever comes to your mind. Here's the word: "Politics!"

Some of you will no doubt say either "Republican" or "Democrat." Others may say "Government." Maybe you thought of games, partisanship, or broken promises. Still others may have thought of service, honor, and freedom. Whatever your answer, it's a safe guess that it was based on your own personal experience with politics. Your own political alignment and activity, as well as the current political climate, will influence your views. If you or a relative has served in public office may also have an affect.

The point is, we all see the same things, but we see them differently depending on our life's experiences. That's the key. No two people have the exact same life experience, and hence, no two people have the exact same beliefs. It's why one person can see abortion as murder and another person can see it as the mother's right to decide what goes on inside her body. They are conflicting beliefs, to be sure, but they're also different beliefs, each tied to what is written on a Belief Lens. The beliefs on our Belief Lens become the "why" behind what we feel and what we do—in short, how we behave.

It's the wide variety of our prescriptions that makes our world the diverse place that it is. All kinds of people see all kinds of things differently. It's not so much what you're looking at as where you're coming from.

Fast Cars and Rules

To better understand how this concept works, imagine that you've just bought a new sports car and you're out for a drive when you see a sign for a curve up ahead. Because you want to check out just how tight the steering is in your new car, you take the curve wide and fast.

At about the same instant that you realize you can't hold the right lane at the speed you're going, you look up and see a big semitrailer truck coming into the curve from the opposite direction. It's coming right at you! The truck and your car are going to collide unless you do something fast. In an instant, your brain runs through the logical outcome of this situation—you're traveling very fast, your car is smaller than the truck, you're going to collide, that big truck is going to smash your little car. You say something like, "Oh no, I'm going to die!" and then, very quickly, you jerk your steering wheel to the left, slam on the brake, and roll over the embankment, narrowly avoiding the collision. The next thing you know the paramedics have pried you out of your car at the bottom of the ravine and taken you to the hospital where they keep you overnight for observation and in the morning tell you you're banged up and bruised a little, but you're going to be OK.

Now, let's run this imaginary experience through the Belief Paradigm. First of all, which of the four basic needs was being threatened in this situation? Your need to live, right? Your basic I-want-to-survive need. Once the need you were trying to meet was established—and in this case it would have been established very quickly—then what principle was on your Belief Lens concerning big trucks and little cars? Big trucks smash little cars, right?

As we look through our Belief Lens, we begin to formulate principles or rules that shape our perception of any given event. When an event comes through our Belief Lens, we interpret it based upon our past experiences. Our rules surface in the form of "if/then" statements. In your sports car adventure, the rule you applied was, "If big trucks smash little cars, then I'm going to die!" Rules might be thought of as mental responses to the application of our beliefs; and it's our mental responses, or self-talks, that trigger the next phase of the connection—Behavior. (See illustration below.)

Behavior—the Response to Your Belief

Remember what you did. First your brain went through the logical sequence of what would happen next and you deduced, "Oh no, I'm going to die!" Then you swerved and slammed on the brakes. Those were your actions; that was your behavior. Notice that you had a mental, emotional, and physical response prior to your behavior. Your mental response was to consider the outcome of your current situation, and your emotional response was fear, panic, and anxiety. Your physical response was what was going on internally—the influx of adrenaline, the pounding of your heart, the sweating.

It was only after you experienced these mental, emotional, and physical responses that your hands jerked the steering wheel and your foot hit the brake. It was only then that you behaved. There will always be mental, emotional, and physical responses prior to our behaviors and actions. It's important to note at this point that the intensity of mental, emotional, and physical responses is in direct proportion to the perception of what is happening. In this case, since the truck was big and time was of the essence, your mental, emotional, and physical responses were very intense. They screamed: "Do it now!" You responded in kind.

We never respond until we're compelled to respond. Our minds and bodies have an inherent natural tendency toward responses in kind, or, to use the scientific term, toward homeostasis. Homeostasis is the tendency to maintain equilibrium, to stay in a "like" state. A good way to demonstrate homeostasis is to have two people push against each other's hands. When one pushes hard, the other will push back hard. When one hardly pushes at all, the other will hardly push at all. Intuitively, both people are maintaining equilibrium, or homeostasis.

Our body's reactions to outside temperature changes also help illustrate this tendency toward homeostasis. If your body gets hot, what does it do? It sweats. Sweat cools the body. If it gets cold, what does it do? It shivers. Shivering warms the body. The objective behind both functions is to maintain normal body temperature, or to maintain homeostasis. We don't have to sit and think about it. Our bodies adjust automatically to physical stimuli.

In like manner, we will similarly respond to any and all outside mental stimuli with first mental then emotional and physical responses. Most mental stimuli aren't as simple as a drop or rise in temperature. They require interpretation—we must perceive what they mean. The greater the perceived pressure or threat, the stronger our mental, emotional, and physical responses are going to be. Unlike our body's natural response to, say, hot and cold, our response to life's daily events is based upon a perception that may or may not be a physical reality. The intensity of our responses will always be in direct proportion to our perception of the intensity of the threats (regardless of how great or small the reality). The greater the perception of a threat, the greater the response will be. Do you know anyone who overreacts? Why? Because their perception of what's going on is greater than the reality. And to what is our perception anchored? Directly to our Belief Lens, of course. Perception is always going to be based on the beliefs we've formed through our life experiences.

Our mental, emotional, and physical responses, then, determine our behavior all within the structure created by our beliefs. If our Belief Lens is clouded with negative beliefs, then our responses will also be negative, just as positive beliefs lead to positive responses. Those responses have a physical price attached to them.

Let's return to our sports car example, but we'll change the circumstances just a bit. This time, when you come speeding around the corner, instead of seeing a big truck you see a police car parked on the side of the road. As you fly past the officer, you see that he has his radar gun trained on you. While your life may not be threatened like it was with the big truck, your response is still, nonetheless, very similar. Your body releases adrenaline, your heart rate spikes, and you're suddenly feeling very stressed. This is the short-term, immediate response to the stimuli. Once the danger subsides, your body will return to homeostasis.

What happens next—aside from the ticket, of course—is going to depend largely on your perception of the situation. What does that ticket mean to you? Will the ticket haunt your thoughts for the next few days, weeks, or months? Does the ticket mean that your insurance rates will go up, which means that you won't be able to afford to make the payments on your new car, which means that it will be repossessed, your credit score will be ruined, and your spouse will hate you now?

Or is that ticket an opportunity for you to learn and grow? Sure, you'll have to pay the consequences, but now you know better. You'll be a safer driver from now on. And thank goodness that police officer was there to help keep the neighborhood safe, because, after all, you really were going too fast.

In these two responses, what are the long-term effects? Allowing the negative thoughts to run free in your mind will increase your stress levels, which causes your body to release the stress hormone cortisol. Now, rather than returning to homeostasis, your body is caught up in a hormonal imbalance (we'll talk more about the price of this imbalance in Chapter 5).

If you've heard the statement, "Weighing on your mind," that's what we're talking about here. Your belief window allows things to weigh on your mind, keeping them constantly in your view; your body pays the price.

What is the result of the more positive reaction? Most likely you'll return to homeostasis. Your body will thank you for that positive approach.

These outcomes are all triggered by your beliefs. Mental, emotional, and physical responses to situations are going to happen; there's not really anything you can do to stop them. How you perceive those responses, however, is based on your Belief Lens. Your perception of the responses, in turn, affects your life. The good news is that you can control your perception by changing the prescription on your Belief Lens with new beliefs.

Consequences

This brings us to the final phase of the Belief Paradigm—the Results phase. (See illustration below.) In the results phase, we find out what

the consequences are of our behaviors. Going back to the automobile accident, what were your consequences as a high-speed sports car driver who took the corner too fast? A trip to the hospital, medical bills, higher insurance rates, and you had to go out and buy another car, right? All those were results, or consequences, of the crash. But look at what else happened. You lived, that's what happened. That's the result we want to look at as we plug the hypothetical sports car experience into the Belief Paradigm; that's the result we want to connect to the Needs Quadrants. Only by connecting our results to our needs are we able to accurately conclude whether the results of our behavior truly meet our needs. In the sports car example, the need that was being threatened was your need to live, and, since in the end you indeed lived, you satisfied your need. Since the results of your behavior satisfied your need, that means your belief, "Big trucks smash little cars," worked. It is, for you, an empowering belief—one that makes you stronger or more confident. You can safely make that determination. Making a hard left turn and crashing to the bottom of the hill was the right choice. It was preferable to a head-on collision with a big truck. However, notice there was also a hindering belief at work here, or a belief that could impede your ability to progress. Did speeding meet any need? No! The belief that it's OK to speed hurt the need to live because speeding unnecessarily cost the driver monetarily as well as physically. It's preferable to not have those expenses and injuries.

The exciting part about the Belief Paradigm is that it can be applied to all areas of life. Through it we can identify those beliefs on our Belief Lens that drive the kind of behavior that produces results that satisfy our needs—beliefs that work for us. We can also identify those beliefs that drive behavior that doesn't work for us—in other words, behavior that produces results that do not satisfy our needs.

Laws to Live By

To help with that identifying process, there are two significant Natural Laws I want to share with you. By Natural Laws, I mean guiding principles that we can put in place that we know will drive productive behavior. Here are a couple of facetious examples: "Never fry bacon naked" and "Don't get in fights with ugly people—they have nothing to lose." The Golden Rule qualifies as a Natural Law: "Do unto others as you would have them do unto you." That's just another example. You can call them truths or values or standards or words of wisdom, if you like. The point is, Natural Laws are always applicable.

The first Natural Law the is:

When the results of my behavior meet my needs, there is an empowering belief on my Belief Lens.

It can be helpful if you circle the word "my" in this Natural Law. That's because we want to emphasize that we're talking about "my" behavior, "my" needs, "my" Belief Lens. This is an individual thing. Everyone will have different personal truths. Personal truths are not good or bad. They're not right or wrong. They're empowering or hindering depending on whether they drive behavior that meets our needs. Not our neighbor's needs, our needs. As we use the Belief Paradigm to analyze our personal truths, we want to find the beliefs that work for us and that empower us—and the only reason they'll be empowering is if they drive behavior that meets our own individual needs. We'll be the only true judge of that.

Again, what are personal truths? They're our beliefs. They're the values we've assigned to all those things we come in contact with in our lives. They govern our actions. They are what motivate us and drive our behavior.

Let's use the example of Community Commerce. A vital practice in Community Commerce is holding home meetings where invited guests learn more about a company's products and opportunity. Yet, despite this meeting being so essential to a successful business, many distributors do not hold these meetings. This is a prime example of how the beliefs on our Belief Lens drive how we behave. Let's take the example of someone who never holds home meetings despite recognizing their importance. The reason for the reluctance to hold home meetings is the belief on the person's lens that says, "Home meetings won't work for me because no one will come. My time is better spent doing other, more productive things."

With that belief in place, let's start with the distributor initially considering holding a home meeting and run this example through the

Belief Paradigm. What will be the behavior of the person who has a "no one will attend my home meetings" belief on his or her Belief Lens? We can easily imagine that behavior since we know it's going to be consistent with the belief. We can therefore imagine that typically it will involve half-hearted efforts to invite people (if any effort at all), low commitment and enthusiasm level for holding the event, and a belief that the meeting's failure is already a foregone conclusion.

We can also safely imagine that such behavior might lead to a reluctance to discuss holding home meetings with either that distributor's upline or downline, and, quite likely, a readiness to blame any slump in the business on the system rather than on personal effort. Now, by connecting these results back to the Needs Quadrants, we can determine if the need trying to be fulfilled is in fact being met. In this case, what need is driving the belief that "no one will attend my home meeting"? Possible scenarios are:

1. The self-esteem need—when no one comes to my home meeting, I'll feel rejected and worthless.

2. Need to live—since no one will come to my meeting, I'll be wasting precious time that I could be doing something else, something more productive.

3. The need to enjoy—I don't have time to do all the fun things I want to do already, so wasting time on a meeting that's just going to be a failure anyway is pointless.

4. Love need—if my friends don't come when I invite them to this meeting, our relationship will be damaged and it will be awkward the next time we get together.

Later in the book, we'll go through a more systematic, step-by-step process to show you how to determine which of your needs are being threatened.

No matter which of the needs is most threatened, the question is, "Do the results of the behavior meet the need or needs?"

The answer in this case is quite obviously, "No." Failure to do the things that lead to success won't contribute to satisfying any need, let alone all of them. Since the results do not satisfy the needs, what does that say about the belief driving the behavior that produces those results? It is a hindering belief.

A hindering belief should always be changed, of course, to an empowering belief—to a belief that drives behavior that produces results that satisfy needs.

How about a new home meeting belief that says, "Home meetings can be challenging, but they are important. They give me the chance to share something truly valuable with people that I care about"? With this new belief in place, it's easy to imagine resultant behavior that will include enthusiasm, commitment, and hard work—the results of which will be a growing and thriving business. This doesn't mean that every one you invite to a meeting will come or that every meeting will be a walk in the park. What it does mean is that the new belief will drive behavior that will create opportunities for increased productivity and better relationships with others—behavior that would in turn produce results that would potentially satisfy parts of all four needs.

We can, and should, put all of our beliefs to the reality test. Let's take another hypothetical example, and I'll use myself this time. In my work with MonaVie I'm on the road a lot, conducting seminars and giving speeches. I enjoy my work. Let's say that I have a belief on my Belief Lens that says, "Henry, if you teach a great seminar or give a great speech, you deserve a reward." That's my truth. That's what I believe. Let's say I give my audience what I think is a terrific experience. I go back to my hotel room, and I say to myself, "Great job today. You deserve a reward." So I pick up the phone and say, "Cheesecake please," and, before long, room service brings me a big piece of cheesecake with chocolate and strawberries on top. I eat that cheesecake and feel wonderful because I did a great job; now my hunger's satisfied and I'm doing just fine.

The questions I have to ask myself as they relate to the first Natural Law are these: Is there an empowering belief on my Belief Lens? Did the results of my behavior meet my needs?

And the answer is…"I don't know yet."

It's too soon to tell. Yes, I'm comfortable right now, and my appetite is taken care of today. But I'll need to eat cheesecake every day for a year or more to really know if this behavior is meeting my needs. Which brings us to our second Natural Law, which says:

Results take time to measure.

Do our results meet our needs over time? Is what we're doing a quick fix or is it a satisfying solution? Does it work over the long haul? As we observe our behavior, we don't want to focus on short-term, isolated instances; we want to focus on our habitual responses, on satisfying a lasting need.

I remember making a conscious decision to cut down on my office hours when I began to ask myself this question: Ten years from now, what will I be glad I did today? Ask yourself that question and you'll really begin to look at results over time, at the long-term impact of your behavior and not at short-term fixes. I remember that my ski days went up dramatically after I asked myself that "ten-year" question. So did my emphasis on my family, my work, my health, and all the other areas of my life I care most about. I was able to put office hours in proper perspective. I realized that I want to live life fully, and I want to have a lot of enriching and rewarding experiences. I started creating those experiences and taking advantage of opportunities, because I know I'm going to regret it if I don't. I planned trips with my children to have memorable experiences together. I got in the habit of finding out where they wanted to go, what their interests were, and what they found important. I began to coordinate my business trips to also facilitate family outings. I realized my children would be grown and gone in a decade or so, and now is my only chance to build "bricks on the wall" with them. Further, I realized my need to enjoy. There were things I wanted to do in my life, and if I wasn't careful, the optimum time for doing them would pass me by.

Without plugging "over time" into my focus, I wouldn't have planned trips that could satisfy so many of my needs or orchestrated any number of other experiences I determined to be important to me. Those two small words—"over time"—have the capability of giving us a new perspective on our lives, a perspective that enables us to put our priorities in their proper order. They are essential in helping us identify empowering beliefs.

It's only when we view our actions in the context of the long run that we can enjoy all the benefits of perspective. Short-term solutions just won't do. It's long-term results that matter, and we'll have the patience to wait for them.

A Different Point of View

The life of Edward Joseph Flanagan serves as a good illustration of what I'm talking about. When he was a young priest, the Catholic church sent Flanagan far from his native land of Ireland to its archdiocese in Omaha, Nebraska. In Omaha, Flanagan became acquainted with several troubled youngsters. In deciding how best to deal with these boys, Flanagan determined that they could be rehabilitated if, instead of going off to a prisonlike facility, they could be raised in a community that taught them proper rules and values.

The priest had a belief that, "There is no such thing as a bad boy."

In 1917, he boarded five of these juvenile delinquents in an old rundown house he rented in Omaha, where he allowed the boys to govern themselves. Over time, that rented house became a 1,300-acre community that gained its own incorporation. It was officially called Boys Town, and its founder, Father Flanagan, became its most famous resident—so famous that in 1938 the Hollywood movie *Boys Town* won a best acting Oscar for Spencer Tracy, who starred as Father Flanagan.

If Father Flanagan hadn't joined his principle—"There is no such thing as a bad boy"—with the perspective of "over time," Boys Town would never have happened. He chose to spend his time pursuing what he knew would bring him peace and satisfaction. He satisfied his needs and did a lot of boys a lot of good.

Looking Back Helps

Referring to the survey that began this chapter, you may find it interesting to know that none of the four thousand retired executives questioned said they wished they'd spent more time at the office. Not one! Their top two answers: 1) making better use of your time through identifying values and goals, and 2) taking better care of your health, also reflect the two nonrenewable assets we have in our lives (time and health). Once they are gone you can't get them back.

When you're 70 or on your deathbed, what will you wish you'd done? What beliefs will you wish you'd placed on your Belief Lens? What needs will you wish you'd taken better care of? Start taking care of them now!

Instant Replay

Key Points

- We all have needs.

- Our needs fit into four categories: the need to live, to love, to enjoy, and to feel self-esteem.

- Our beliefs strive to satisfy our needs by the behavior they drive. Empowering beliefs drive behavior that satisfactorily meets our needs over time. Hindering beliefs drive behavior that does not satisfactorily meet our needs over time and keep us from reaching our personal best.

• The Belief Paradigm provides a way to identify all of the above.

Personal Exercises

• Review the last situation in which you felt stress. What was the need that drove that stress response?

• Make a list of as many hindering beliefs that you can recognize. Identify the needs that drive those hindering beliefs.

Where Do We Go from Here?

In chapter two, we'll look at how we get our personal truths and why our hindering beliefs can be so hard to get rid of.

CHAPTER TWO

BLAME IT ON THIRD GRADE

Many of our principles are imprinted when we're still in grade school—and you thought you didn't learn anything in the third grade! It's the third grader in us that is driving most areas of our lives today.

It sounds simple enough, this idea of achieving our personal best through principle-driven behavior. Plug in correct principles, behave accordingly, and voilà! Our results meet our needs, and we live happily ever after.

Well, the truth is, it is that simple.

But it isn't that easy.

A lot of the reason is because of third grade.

I'm being facetious here, but only to a point, and only to make a point. I want you to think back to the third grade when the teacher gathered the whole class in a circle and announced it was time for art. I'm willing to wager that based on what happened there determined what you think of yourself as an artist to this day.

What happened probably went something like this: The teacher said, "OK class, everybody get out your crayons and drawing paper." So you got out your crayons and your drawing paper and then the teacher said, "Here's a picture of a boat; everyone draw this boat." You finished drawing your boat, looked down at your boat, looked up at the teacher's boat, looked back down at your boat, looked at the teacher's boat again, and you thought, "Doesn't look like the teacher's boat...I can't draw!" Then your friends came by and looked at your boat, snickered, and said, "Doesn't look like the teacher's boat," and you thought, "I can't draw!"

Then the teacher took all the boats and hung them up on the walls of the room. Every day for two weeks you got to walk into that room and see your boat, and every time you saw it you thought to yourself, "I can't draw! I wish the teacher would take the pictures down. I'm so embarrassed." So I ask you today if you can draw, and you say, "No! You ought to see the boat I drew in the third grade. It stunk! I can't draw!"

And guess what? You never tried again. Why didn't you try again? Because through a traumatic experience one of your four basic needs was threatened when you were in the third grade, that's why. Which need was it? The self-esteem need. You were embarrassed. You decided you could do without feeling that way in your life. You didn't want to be embarrassed any more. So whenever art came up after that, what did you do? You got out of it or you hid your drawing or you made fun of your drawing before everyone else could have the chance. Every time you did that, you strengthened your belief that you couldn't draw! You made that belief stronger and stronger and stronger, and you've gone on strengthening it your whole life.

Imprints and Synapses

Do you realize that in some very real ways, it's the third grader in you that's still driving you today? Is that a scary thought? The third grader in you drives you because you shaped your beliefs and your opinions and your perceptions of who you are back then. More important, from that day forward you have sought to validate your beliefs and experiences. It's your truth, your reality. It's your security blanket. In short, it is all you have. It's you! Life is a process of validating life's experiences and beliefs.

That makes it hard to change.

The strengthening of a belief such as, "I can't draw," isn't just a figure of speech, either. It isn't wholly intangible. It is an actual physiological process that medical science calls imprinting. It's through imprinting that we record our beliefs, our life's experiences. We have five senses and anytime one of those five senses brings in information, it's imprinted—or recorded—on the brain. This is done by a transmission through hundreds of millions of brain cells called neurons. Every time we have a thought, every time we have an experience, it's neurologically recorded between the neurons. Scientists have studied the process and have identified the spaces in which electrical/chemical signals pass. They're called synapses. We all have hundreds of millions of synapses that have been created to facilitate the need for neurological transfer.

Further, science tells us we all have the capacity to create new synapses for additional neurological transfers. The more experiences we have, the more synapses we bring into play; the more we validate those experiences, the stronger the imprints become. In the third-grade art class example, the moment we compared our crummy boat with the teacher's terrific boat, we created a synapse, or route, for an imprint to travel that said, "I can't draw!" Every time we looked at, or thought about, our boat after that, we made our imprint stronger and stronger. We reinforced it. Much like constantly walking the same route in the mountains turns a path into a trail, so does constant reinforcement turn our imprints into well-worn passages, and that translates to rock-solid beliefs. (Of course, I should note that I realize many have had experiences just the opposite. The teacher said, "You can draw!" and everyone admired your boat. To this day your imprint from that positive experience no doubt reinforces your art talent.)

Why We Do What We Do

In many instances, we may not even be consciously aware of the synapse trails that date back to our formative years. But rest assured they are firmly planted, well traveled, and in excellent working order. The principles that created them in the first place are solidly on our Belief Lens. They shape the way we think and the way we see and eventually the way we behave. They can be called up anytime, anywhere, through all the senses. Smelling creates powerful imprints. I remember walking through the streets of San Francisco, and as I passed by a corner market I smelled something that instantly put me in a good mood. It took me a moment to place the smell. Then I realized they were tuberoses. At my high school junior prom that's what I'd given my date: tuberoses. When I smelled them I was immediately back in Hawaii, at the high school prom.

It's easy to underestimate the power of our early experiences—of what happened in third grade. I once met a lady who related during a seminar her own third-grade experience. She was in Germany as a young girl because her father was working there. She and her older brother were enrolled in a German school where no English was spoken. Because the administration thought she was older than her brother, who was in second grade, she was put in the third grade instead of first grade.

So here she was a first-grader in a third-grade class—where they spoke no English!

There was an assignment to copy material off the front chalkboard that she didn't understand. She didn't know what to do and struggled communicating with the German schoolteacher. As the teacher's frustration mounted, she finally rapped the little girl on the knuckles for not doing the assignment right.

The mix-up was soon discovered and she was sent back to the first grade where she belonged, but the memory of that experience was not erased. As an adult, this woman still admitted to a fear that she wouldn't perform correctly all the assignments of her job and would do something wrong. She was still being driven by that powerful imprint made when she was just starting elementary school.

Time Equals Strength

Over time, of course, our imprints—empowering or hindering—only get stronger through validation. The stronger our beliefs become, the more powerfully they drive our thoughts and actions. Our behavior will reflect what we believe. Let's say, by way of example, that you were raised in a Republican family. Your dad was a Republican. Your mom was a Republican. Every time there was a presidential election they gathered you around the television and said, "I hope the Republicans win." They may have even had a sign in the front yard advocating a Republican candidate. All your life you heard them talk positively about Republicans. So you have this belief that Republicans are good and Democrats aren't so good. As you go out into the world, you get some information that says the Republicans did something well, and what do you say to yourself? "I knew it, that's what mom and dad said. Right on. Way to go. Republicans are good," and you strengthen, or validate, your imprint, your belief.

On the other hand, if you get some equally valid information that says the Democrats did something well, what do you say to yourself? You probably say, "It's a fluke. They're pulling the wool over my eyes. They didn't mean to do it." You discount it because Democrats doing well doesn't match with your reality, your truth, your experience. You push it aside. (Precisely the same process operates if we switch Republican bias to Democrat bias in this hypothetical situation.)

Over time, as two people validate their conflicting truths, they polarize or become further and further apart. They become entrenched in their beliefs. They only see what is true to them. They become blind to everything else. Do you know any hardheaded people? Why are they hardheaded? Because they've validated only their way and have been blind to everything else.

All of us, as members of the human family, not only have roots, but deep roots that drive our behavior because of conditions and events that may have occurred long before we were born.

The culture in which we are raised will unavoidably have a profound impact on how we believe—and behave. We readily adopt the truths of our culture and behave according to those beliefs. Just knowing this goes a long way in explaining human behavior.

Strong Enough to Die For

Consider the phenomenon of Japanese kamikaze pilots in World War II. Thousands of young Japanese airmen, many of them not yet twenty, joined the Kamikaze Corps toward the end of the war when they were encouraged to do so by their leaders. Joining the Kamikaze Corps was the equivalent of signing your own death warrant. It meant that you'd climb into the cockpit of your single-seat fighter plane, usually a Japanese Zero, and purposely dive-bomb into an enemy gunboat in the Pacific Ocean.

More than fifteen hundred of these suicide missions were carried out, and nearly a hundred Allied ships were sunk, before the Japanese surrendered and the war was ended. In America, these suicide raids were unfathomable. But not in Japan. Because the age-old Japanese code of warfare viewed defeat as unthinkable and shameful, it made sense to pull out all the stops when subjugation appeared imminent. Suicide was seen as an acceptable weapon in the context of that culture. The name "kamikaze" was borrowed from a victorious chapter in Japan's military history—when the samurai warriors turned back invading Mongol troops in the late 1200s, the effort was aided greatly by what the Japanese believe were divine winds. The name they gave them was kamikaze winds. It was an honor to be a kamikaze pilot, and those who volunteered believed that by giving their life for their country, they would have honor in their next life.

That's how strong our imprints can become, formed by the beliefs that drive them.

History is full of examples of unswerving devotion to cultural truths, just as it's full of unswerving devotion to truths that we acquire from other sources.

The point is, we're suited with our truths very early on, some of them even before we're born. They begin shaping us from childhood. We inherit them from our culture, our parents, our environment. Some we acquire ourselves. Whatever the source, the more reinforcement we give these beliefs, the stronger they become, and the stronger our synapses become.

I Can Run!

When I was young, my development as a runner was based on a subconscious belief that could best be defined as, "Winning beats sitting on the bench." Looking back, I realize that it was by following this belief that I wound up competing in a sport I otherwise might not have been attracted to.

Running was not my first sport of choice. I had grown up in Texas, and until I was fourteen years old I wasn't going to be the next Jim Ryun, I was going to be the next Roger Staubach. Football was king, and the Dallas Cowboys were royalty. In the ninth grade I was captain and quarterback of my junior high school football team in Richardson, a suburb of Dallas. Life might have been one long bed of roses after that except for one small problem: the 1968 season. The football team I quarterbacked didn't win a single game. We played ten games and lost them all. Still, I thought I was a pretty good quarterback who would only get better. In one game I completed all four of the four passes I threw. But my friends pointed out to me that three of them were to the other team.

When basketball season came along I played that sport, too. In the pecking order of Texas schoolboy sports, basketball ranked number three, right behind football and spring football. I had practiced jump shots in my driveway since I was a little kid, and I was deadly accurate, hence my assignment as captain and starting shooting guard on the ninth-grade team.

Then a truly unfortunate and, when you think about it, ironic event occurred in my life. You know how teenagers are prone to growth spurts that burst out of the blue, between dinner the night before and breakfast the next morning? Such a growth spurt hit me in late December of 1968. At the last basketball practice before Christmas break I was five-foot-four. At the first basketball practice after Christmas break I was five-foot-seven. Normally such an increase in height would be construed as the single greatest event in a basketball player's life. Now I could post up the five-four guys. But there was a catch. My shot was thrown off completely. I couldn't shoot the lights out anymore. Casting away with my combination throwing/shooting delivery was now sending the ball clanging hard off the glass. The good news was I was taller and stronger and in a position to become a better shooter once I adjusted and worked at it. The bad news was I wasn't starting any more. I went to the end of the bench and died there.

Which brought about…track season. I had never been anything other than average at the races we ran in gym classes, and the longest distance I'd ever run was 660 yards. There was no serious track and field background in my family, no foreshadowing of talent. In the aforementioned pecking order of Texas schoolboy sports, track and field checked in with a status just behind football and basketball. So, as a fourteen-year-old, I ran.

Wendell Harding, my junior high track coach, wasn't nicknamed the Drill Sergeant but he could have been. His idea of a good workout was two good workouts. He thrived on the sight of teenage bodies in various stages of collapse after repeat intervals and three-hour workouts. He set about whipping his teams into the best shape they could imagine (and in some cases that they couldn't imagine). If there was any talent anywhere, Coach Harding's philosophy was that it would come to the surface once you got all the rust out of the way. I remember only too well the ten-mile runs he'd put us through on the old dirt track behind our junior high school. I'd shower and limp home and be really sore and not sure if I wanted to do that again. Then the next day I'd do it again.

As a result, I discovered that I had an ability to run fairly fast for a fairly long time. By the time the Richardson School District finals came around that spring, I entered the 1,320 (a race just short of a mile), and, in addition to winning the race, I set a new district record. I had never been so thrilled—or rewarded—by anything I'd done in athletics in my young life. Everybody else came in behind me. The line formed behind Henry. It felt terrific.

My family moved from Dallas to Corpus Christi the next year, and what sports do you think I went out for at Corpus Christi King High School? Football and basketball? Hardly. I opted for the sports I had success in. I'd grown to really like winning. The first day of school I met with the track coach, James Blackwood, to plot my course of action for the year. I ran cross-country in the fall and was on the track team in the spring. What was the most fun wasn't nearly as important as what was the most successful. Think about it. What's more fun: shooting baskets or running laps? Trust me. Take my word for it. Shooting baskets is a lot more fun. In fact, what was the punishment for the basketball players who missed their baskets? Running laps, right? So what did I do? I went straight to the punishment. Why? Because I was the best at the punishment.

I was seventh in the Texas State cross-country championships as a sophomore and in the mile at the state meet the following spring I was seventh again. We moved to Hawaii for my junior year of high school and by then you couldn't have stopped me from running with all the surfboards on Waikiki Beach. Running fast was my ticket to self-esteem and popularity, to dates with good-looking girls, to trophies and ribbons and congratulatory pats on the back. That was my perception. That's what drove me.

I was fortunate to attend Punahou High School where, under the guidance of coach Al Rowan, I kept making improvements and beating people. After six state titles while in Hawaii, I got comfortable with what they call the "spoils of victory." I had plenty of imprints that said I was successful because of all the people who came in after I did at the end of a race.

Senility—The Only Way Out

I'd developed all these imprints and their corresponding synapses that said, "Winning is number one." At the time, if I had known what a synapse was, I might have asked this key question: Once they've been made, can we get rid of our imprints? But sadly, I'd have learned that while the answer is, "Yes, there is a way," it would not have been a satisfactory remedy. That's because the only way to get rid of our imprints is with senility. When a person goes senile the synapses that carry imprints actually break down.

So where does that leave us? If there's no other way we can break an imprint that's been strengthened and reinforced over a lifetime (and there isn't), how can we ever change our beliefs (and still keep our minds)?

Again, the answer is simple to understand… but hard to do.

The solution is to use a new synapse to make a new imprint. If I want to be a good artist after years of telling myself, "I can't draw!" then I have to form a new belief. I need to take art lessons. I need to learn to draw. I need to get in touch with the fundamentals. I need to practice and listen to teachers and fellow students who tell me I have the makings of a good artist. In short, I need to have new experiences—new experiences that reinforce my new belief. As I get better and better and as I listen to positive reinforcement, it's possible to establish a new imprint that is actually stronger than the old one. When that happens, and I'm asked if I can draw, I'll say, "Yeah, I can draw. You ought to see this house I just drew. Everybody liked it. I'm a good artist."

Likewise, if I want to be a runner who looks at his own results and not the results of others, I need to keep saying, "Doing my best and giving my all is what's important," over and over again—until that imprint is stronger than the one that says, "Winning is the only thing."

Again, it won't be easy. We are a product of our life experiences, the sum total of our imprints, and most psychologists agree that by age five, or age seven at the latest, our personalities have largely been shaped. Our early imprints are our strongest imprints. That means that we're naturally going to perpetuate the beliefs of our parents and the third grade for the rest of our lives—that is, unless and until those beliefs bring us too much pain. When the change looks less painful than the pain, then we'll seek out alternatives, but not until then.

Or, and this is an important distinction, we can recognize the ability we have to create new imprints that can overtake those old imprints we'd like to supplant—the ones that haven't been all that positive in our lives. We can do this before pain forces us to. Misery and suffering are not prerequisites to change. We don't have to hurt first. The pain doesn't have to get to the point that we consider it unbearable.

Positive Imprinting

I should add here that many imprints are valuable. Many of them are keepers. We're lucky, of course, if our early lives were filled with positive imprinting. If our boat looked like the teacher's boat we could have saved a lot of time and energy.

I was lucky to have a lot of positive imprinting at a young age. I can remember my father going out of his way to give me experiences that would shape me and make me hungry for life. In the fourth grade, I can vividly recall when he took me to Brazil. He was doing some work down there and he took my brother and me with him. I remember going to the Copacabana and to the Iguaçu Falls. My dad rented a plane with a friend so we could fly directly over the falls. When we came back we purposely took a flight that stopped in every Central American country. Why? Because he wanted to give us that experience. I remember stopping at the Panama Canal, just so we could see it. He believed you're only as good and as rich as your experiences, and he passed that belief on to his family. It's been a positive imprint for me my entire life. That's one imprint, or a series of imprints, that I would never want to override.

I was also fortunate to grow up in an environment that stressed the importance of always being involved in a good cause. I've spent my life chasing goals. If it wasn't a gold medal or a law degree it was developing a seminar or trying to run a four-minute mile. The more I've learned about imprinting, the more I've analyzed why I'm the way I am—if anything, I'm an overachiever. I can trace it back to my parents, who always said that anything is possible. That was the family motto. They were the kind of parents who didn't act surprised if their kids got good grades. We didn't get rewarded for getting A's in school. There was this expectation of excellence, and that was what got imprinted. When I was young, my mother gave me a quote from my grandfather, Henry D. Moyle, which I have always kept. He said: "You can accomplish anything of a righteous nature if you have the faith, the desire, and are willing to do the work."

Creatures of Habit

When I look back on it further, my early experiences as a runner also help show just how strong our third-grade imprints can be; how they can relegate us to our places in life. I remember how easy it was, after a few races, to size up the field before a race and be able to predict fairly accurately where everyone would finish. We tended to be creatures of habit. So often we'd mirror the results of our earlier races, myself included. I would finish in front of the people I always finished in front of and in back of those I tended to finish in back of. Very often, we pigeonhole ourselves because of our imprints. I'd look at a person I'd beaten in five straight races, and I had no problem at all thinking I would beat that person the next time we raced as well. But when it came to runners who had beaten me in the past, I had a lot of trouble thinking that this time the result would be different. I'd want the result to be different, of course, and I'd hope it would be different, but that's not what my imprint was screaming. My imprint said the results wouldn't be different, and often that would result in a self-fulfilling prophecy.

If we dwell on it, we can find many specific instances in our lives that gave us the beliefs that drive our behaviors. I remember working with a policewoman in one of my seminars who talked about her obsessiveness to overachieve. She took on an enormous number of projects in her life, and she had to be perfect at all of them. She expected nothing less of herself.

When I took her through the Belief Paradigm and had her think about what life experiences she might have had that made her that way, she had an interesting response. She said both of her parents were alcoholics who often ran away and abandoned her when she was young; they couldn't keep a job and failed at most everything they tried to do. She watched this as a child and developed a belief system that if you weren't perfect that's how you'd turn out. That became the belief on her Belief Lens. In response to that belief, she didn't just turn into an achiever, she turned into an overachiever. She would not let herself relax, ever. She was so afraid of failure that she became a perfectionist. That was her security blanket. With the help of the Belief Paradigm, she was able to see that in order to make life easier, if she decided that was her goal, she would have to effect a change in her belief system, and to do that she'd have to create an abundance of new imprints.

The Advertising Age

Another area that is responsible for a good deal of our imprinting, and one we're often not consciously aware of, is advertising. From an early age, we're susceptible to advertisements. We hear slogans, we see images, we hum jingles, we even smell perfume samples in magazines that come to our homes. Advertising is everywhere. Advertisers know what works; they know how to drive us. That's their business.

Well, this can be good, or it can be not so good. Advertising can give us imprints that are associated with empowering beliefs—remember, empowering beliefs are ones that meet our needs over time—or it can give us imprints that are associated with hindering beliefs. We have to be careful. That's why getting in touch with our beliefs is so valuable. If we really know what drives us and where our imprints come from, we can keep the empowering ones and discard the hindering ones. Advertising is capable of generating positive behavior and results. Take Nike's slogan, "Just Do It," for example. It's not difficult to assume that that message is responsible for people reaching their goals and satisfying their self-esteem need. Even if its original intent was just to sell shoes, "Just Do It" can inspire good imprints.

But advertising can be a double-edged sword. The same ads that inspired some youngsters to "Just Do It" and reach their athletic goals might have inspired other youngsters to rob and, in some instances, kill for the shoes being advertised. "Just Do It" might have had an entirely different imprint on these young people and driven entirely different behavior.

The point is, we are constantly being bombarded by imprint-making material, in one form or another. Once formed, the imprints create amazingly strong personal truths. We should take care to understand what those truths or beliefs are.

Accurate Predictions

Imprinting not only makes it possible for us to predict our own behavior well before an event occurs, but if we know what's on others' Belief Lenses, we can predict their behavior as well. In hiring new employees, companies that attempt to learn about the life experiences of prospective employees have an excellent chance of knowing what kind of employees they're getting. If you know what's important to a person, what they believe about things and what drives them, then it follows that you'll also develop excellent insight into how they're going to act. Their behavior is going to stay true to their imprints and their beliefs. They're going to act according to those life experiences that created those imprints.

On the other side of that coin, if you first observe a person's behavior patterns, you can go backward and fairly accurately predict what their beliefs are. It's behavior that provides us a view into a person's Belief Lens and principles.

For example, if someone is approached with the invitation to join the Community Commerce opportunity but rejects it before learning any of the detail, you not only already know that that's his behavior pattern, but that it's following a belief, because beliefs drive behavior. While you may not be able to completely define that person's belief without more insight, you can be reasonably sure that chances are good the behavior will continue. The negative response to Community Commerce behavior will continue until there is a change of belief.

Behavior doesn't just happen. It's largely internally driven. External events don't have nearly the impact on behavior as imprints that have been established over long years of work and effort. Behavior perpetuates itself and will continue to perpetuate itself—unless and until there's a change in beliefs.

If someone with a history of building successful home-based businesses shows interest in becoming a distributor for a network marketing company, you can be practically certain that they'll put forth the effort to build a successful distributorship. Distributors could make their lives a lot easier by subscribing to that one standard.

In the corporate world, I've noticed that in many companies one of the chief concerns among employees has to do with bosses not treating them with what they perceive as respect. It's a very frustrating issue for a lot of people. If you think about it, it's not hard to predict what's on the Belief Lens of bosses or supervisors who show little respect to those they supervise—even when you've never met them. They probably grew up in an environment where the belief was that bosses are supposed to be authoritative, hands-off supervisors. Bosses aren't supposed to get close to their employees or work directly with them. Their word is gold, their edicts are law, their commands supreme, that kind of thing.

It's quite possible this might have been learned from military service, or such beliefs might also have been learned in homes where men were kings who ruled the house. They got to delegate all the chores. They had little or no hands-on responsibility. That's the belief they grew up with. It's what they know. As a result, there's a lot of old-style management because that's the way a lot of bosses were raised.

Knowing this about your boss won't change your boss, but understanding the imprints and the beliefs behind them can make for a lot healthier outlook than simple resentment. Our imprints aren't just individual-oriented, either. Continuing in the corporate world for a minute, think about the beliefs people have about companies. There are beliefs about work ethic, dress standards, how often meetings should be held, acceptable limits of productivity, and who should park where. You name it. The list goes on and on. Some of these beliefs are in writing in company mission statements and employee manuals. But most are not. They belong to the area of, "That's just the way things are done around here." Are they all true, and are they all healthy? Probably not. Some usually are, and, in fact, often most of these beliefs are good. But some might not be.

Taking a Chance

A good example of this came from a training director I worked with who had a company belief firmly imprinted that said she worked till 6:30 every night because, "That's the way things are done around here." Everyone else did, so she did, too.

Working that late caused her continual concern and distress because she had family needs that she knew were being neglected as a result. Her family needed her before 6:30. Finally, she came up with a new belief that said, essentially, "My work and my family have to be in better balance." To that end, she decided that she would work till 5:30 every night, and then she would leave to take care of her family commitments.

With some fear and trepidation, she tried out her new belief. She would leave work at 5:30 and announce that she had family commitments. Do you know what happened? Nobody said a word. Nobody questioned her. She'd been driven by a perceived company belief that wasn't necessarily true. It turned out it wasn't written in stone. She believed she had to conform to it, so she did. Reexamination allowed her to develop a new, and healthier, belief and imprint.

Similar situations pop up in network marketing. Many times, distributors will succumb to the belief that they have to work their business in a prescribed manner, never deviating or trying anything new. There are many good ideas out there, and assuming that one's upline or mentor is the only source of good ideas can be detrimental to achieving goals. That's not to say that you shouldn't check with and learn from more experienced distributors—especially distributors in your upline. Staying open to possibilities and not subscribing to the belief that because a certain approach worked for someone else means that it is the only way to do business, can save you a lot of trials and difficulties.

Understanding imprinting in the workplace, and the need to look at imprints that are being fueled by hindering beliefs, isn't only one directional. Leaders can benefit greatly from a clear comprehension of imprinting. In my work with Arby's, the fast food company, I watched Steve Sparling, director of corporate training, use the Belief Paradigm to look at employee beliefs that might be changed to make the managers, and in turn the stores, more productive. In one case, after noting that many managers had a tendency to take care of problems by fixing them themselves, he suggested to the supervisors that they should see themselves as being there not to help people do their jobs, but to support them.

Steve is a former weightlifting champion, and he used weightlifting to help explain the difference between helping and supporting. If a weightlifter is trying for a new personal best in, say, the bench press, he never attempts more weight than he's previously lifted unless he has a person called a "spotter." The spotter's purpose is to be there in case the weightlifter can't get the weight back to the bar. Spotters are essential, especially, as we might imagine, in the bench press. Otherwise, a weightlifter trying for a new personal best would have to be successful, or the bar would crush his or her chest and neck.

Steve said he'd never seen anyone even try to do their best lift without a spotter—for the simple reason that they wouldn't attempt to lift heavy weight without someone there to help out. For the same reason, he also said he'd never seen anyone find out their limits and set personal bests without a spotter. The spotter was essential. The spotter had to be there. But the spotter only acted as support. The spotter never got down on the bench and lifted anything until it was absolutely necessary. The spotter's job was to make sure the weight lifter could feel secure enough to go for his best.

Steve told Arby's managers that they need to be spotters, not lifters. To a lot of his managers that meant a new concept—a belief that says to truly be of assistance to others, they need to be supporters, not helpers. They need to adopt an attitude that they'll jump in only when it's necessary, and then only as a support, not as someone who takes over and does the job. It's a new principle designed to drive an entirely different behavior, one that, over time, is designed to better meet the manager's needs as well as the needs of those being managed.

This principle can be easily applied to Community Commerce. Often, uplines take it upon themselves to ensure the success of new distributors that they have signed up. These new distributors are never allowed the opportunity to stretch their own wings and learn how to fly. Eventually, this leads to burn out on the part of the upline and the downline's complete dependency and reliance on that upline. A more effective model would be to be supportive of efforts, offering advice and encouragement, but allowing the new distributor to do their own work. By learning the ropes for themselves, new distributors are more likely to remain active and build a successful business.

On the flip side, there are often uplines that end their involvement with their downline after the signing up process is complete. In effect, they leave new weightlifters to press up that weight alone, without anyone to help if help is needed. While doing the work for a downline member isn't desirable, neither is abandoning them to the wolves. Be there, ready to help if necessary, but allow them to do the work themselves. That's how personal bests are achieved safely and consistently.

No Shortcuts

It's important to understand that developing new imprints takes time and attention. It requires patience. A decision to "turn over a new leaf" doesn't mean it can happen overnight. Nor will it happen merely by meditating or using some other Band-Aid approach. There are no shortcuts or quick fixes to finding new beliefs and building new imprints. Empowering or hindering, imprints need to be respected for the simple reason that they are there. They exist. They represent years and years of reinforcement.

Beliefs and imprints form the lens through which we view the world. This point was dramatically brought home to me after working with Sheila Holzworth of the Principal Financial Group in Des Moines, Iowa. Sheila is a wonderful motivating trainer for Principal Financial. Sheila is also blind. An accident at the age of ten robbed her of her sight, but Sheila was blessed with visionary parents who had prepared her well for the adversity that hit her at a young age. Being visually challenged did not deter her from striving for success and a rewarding life. Her parents, particularly her father, had instilled in Sheila a belief that if you think positively and always aim for the top, you'll get there. The adjustments she made after losing her eyesight meant changing some of her paths. But at the same time, she took care not to eliminate any of her expectations. Her goals remained just as lofty as ever. Sheila loved sports, but now, instead of participating in softball and gymnastics—her two favorite sports before her accident—she chose track. She concentrated specifically on the 100-yard dash, reasoning that a race consisting of one long straightaway was best suited to her capacity.

Sheila adjusted, but she did not change. Her imprints let her keep on "seeing." She lettered in track in high school and also in college, by which point she had added snow and water skiing to her athletic repertoire. In those sports, she managed to go where no blind athlete had ever gone, winning numerous gold medals in national and international competitions while competing for the United States.

Another of this amazing woman's single achievements was when she became the first blind person to climb to the top of 14,410-foot Mount Rainier in Washington. For that accomplishment she was invited to the White House to be honored by President Ronald Reagan. Sheila's account of that climb to the top of Mount Rainier sounds very much like any other person's who has managed that considerable feat. "Believe me, the view from the summit was worth the effort," she told me. "It was a sunny day, the clouds were white and puffy, and the sky was a beautiful blue." She explained that two of her climbing companions who were deaf helped describe the scene to her. "But no one had to tell me how high I was," she said.

Sheila achieved her personal best because she was driven by empowering beliefs. Having positive imprints allowed her to go on despite physical hardships and obstacles. In spite of her handicap, she is a person with uncommon vision.

Once we truly understand that beliefs drive behavior and that our beliefs are not of small construction, but are the result of considerable imprinting, we can then appreciate the enormous work that has gone into building the framework that drives our actions and our attitudes. We can also appreciate why it requires considerable effort to achieve our personal best since we have to overcome imprints that have been around almost as long as we have.

Instant Replay

Key Points

- Imprinting is our brain's way of recording and storing our beliefs.

- Our personal truths are imprinted by five to seven years of age.

- The synapses created by imprinting are like old tires. They can't be destroyed; they can only be replaced by new ones.

- To achieve our personal best, we must overcome hindering beliefs, many of which have been imprinted and reinforced ever since third grade.

Personal Exercise

- Go back to your list of hindering beliefs from chapter one and identify what life experiences created those beliefs.

Where Do We Go from Here?

In chapter three, I'll use a personal story to illustrate the power of imprinting, and what it was that drove me to want to change a hindering belief in order to achieve my personal best.

CHAPTER THREE

IT WORKS!

I experienced the power of principle-driven behavior to achieve my personal best, and so can you!

'd like to pause now and tell you a story—my story. It's about a time in my life when I was driven to change my beliefs, and about what drove me to want to make that change.

It all started the day I quit the college track team.

This was not front-page news. The public outcry was, shall we say, minimal. One gray day in January, after a workout that could best be described as uninspiring, I walked off the track and, with only myself as an audience, announced my "retirement" from the sport. That was that. There was no further discussion about the decision, or, I should add, any disagreement either. The next day, my first as a free man, I decided that my time would be better spent skiing than running.

At the time I was a rather pudgy, semi-out-of-shape twenty-one-year-old college sophomore at Brigham Young University in Provo, Utah.

The way I saw it, my glory days of running were behind me. I was sure that's the way my track coaches (Sherald James and Clarence Robison) at Brigham Young saw it, too. Otherwise I would be on scholarship, which I most decidedly was not.

I ran the steeplechase, a 3,000-meter (approximately two miles) test of endurance around a track. The race includes thirty-five barriers (each three feet high), seven of which have twelve feet of water beyond them. The steeplechase has been described as the track event that most resembles a video game and also life, for that matter (with the obstacles). I hadn't run the steeplechase until my freshman season at BYU when it became my full time event for one very good reason: Nobody good was running it.

Coming out of high school I was a miler, aspiring to be the next Jim Ryun (possibly the greatest miler in history). And not without reason. At Punahou High School in Honolulu, I was the Hawaii state champion twice and ran a 4:18 mile. Punahou named me its Athlete of the Year for 1972 and a number of colleges wrote me recruiting letters. BYU's offer appealed to me most since that's where my brother was attending and because the school is maintained and operated by the church to which I belong. BYU offered me a scholarship and a position on the cross-country and track teams, all of which I gladly accepted.

A Nobody

I was just one of a crowd on the BYU track, and I soon realized that everybody there was a high school hero, too. Everybody had won his state meet or placed really high, and many had won a few national meets for good measure. Talent, competitive drive, and high levels of confidence were everywhere; a whole lot of guys like me, in other words, only more so. I went through the usual freshman culture shock, realizing beating people was going to get harder and harder. I didn't even make the traveling squad for the cross-country team, and when track season rolled around I switched from one of the most popular events, the mile, to one of the most unpopular events, the steeplechase. The coaches thought the steeplechase would give me the opportunity for more success. So did I. But I still didn't letter.

After all that freshman-year indignity came the worst indignity of all: when the coaches encouraged me to interrupt my schooling to serve a two-year church mission. Serving missions isn't unusual for young men in the Mormon faith; in fact, it is quite common, but in the early 1970s, the track coaches at BYU encouraged their best runners to serve their missions after they'd used up their four years of eligibility. They didn't want them to stop running for two years, at the same time piling on weight and a different attitude about sports. They worried that they might come back and not have the same competitive drive.

To me the coaches said, with enthusiasm, "So, Henry, when are you going on your mission?"

I Took a Break

I spent what could have been my sophomore and junior years in Brazil doing my voluntary missionary service. It was a wonderful experience, and I learned many valuable lessons that have served me well in many areas of my life and my worship of God ever since. I have never regretted my two-year "break" in Brazil. But it wasn't exactly high-intensity track training. For two years I rarely ran, except for the occasional sprint to catch the buses in Rio, and I took quite a liking to Brazilian cuisine. I returned to BYU twenty-five pounds heavier and not an inch taller.

I was still officially a member of the track team, but if I wanted my scholarship back I would have to re-earn it. That was the deal. It wasn't going to be easy because during my hiatus two quality steeplechasers had been brought in, one from Mexico and one from Norway. Both were on scholarship and both were faster than me. A lot faster than me. Their times were much lower than my lifetime bests.

I watched my new teammates/rivals in awe. They trained harder than I trained. They had better technique than me, and they both had a lot more experience. I was intimidated. I set about trying to compete with them by training the way they trained and by doing my best to keep pace with their pace. To catch them, I tried to copy them—and I wound up running into nothing but regular doses of discouragement.

What Was I Doing?

Then one day it hit me. Who was I fooling? What was I doing? I no longer had a scholarship. I was in an event behind two runners who did have scholarships and who took delight in beating me every time we trained. What's more, I was older than they were, and I weighed a lot more.

Running wasn't satisfying anymore, or much fun either.

So it was that on a nondescript weekday afternoon during the indoor season in January, I walked away from the field house track and kept on walking, determined to enjoy my new lifestyle, which would include staying up as late as I wanted, eating whatever I wanted, skiing whenever I wanted, and playing intramural basketball.

This mood lasted for almost two weeks.

As I said, my departure from the track team was hardly headline news. No one, least of all the coaches, was even aware I had officially quit. For all they knew, I was still training the same as ever. Certainly, no one begged me to come back. No one asked me to reconsider. No one, that is, except for myself. My parents had always made a point of stressing to my brothers and sisters and me that if you made a commitment then you saw it through to the end, even if the mood you were in when you made the commitment changed (make that especially if the mood you were in when you made the commitment changed). You didn't quit on yourself, in other words. So after I got a few late nights out of my system and a few ski days—strictly taboo for runners on the team—and after I played all the basketball I wanted, I realized I was having a problem facing myself squarely in the mirror.

One More Shot

I'd quit something I'd started, and I knew, instinctively, that if I didn't see the season through to the end, I would regret it. I also knew, somehow, that just going back wouldn't be enough. If I didn't go back and give it my best shot, I would still be disappointed. If I returned and did the best I could with what I had to work with, and saw it through that way to the end, only then could I retire to the couch and the ski slopes with no arguments from within.

So I un-quit. I returned to the team (with the same commotion I'd caused when I left). But this time I had a different attitude. I decided that instead of worrying about how my teammates on scholarship were doing, instead of focusing on their every move and trying to copy their workouts, I would concentrate on getting the most out of myself. Whereas in the past I spent a lot of time wondering if my teammates were healthy, or if they were injured (or wishing they might get injured), or how fast they were running, now my focus was going to be on me. Was I healthy? Was I taking care of myself? Was I getting any faster? How was I doing?

I wasn't going to compare myself to anyone but me.

I became something of a maverick. I drew up my own workout schedules and set my own goals. Personal improvement was my new driving force. I lost weight. I became a toe runner instead of a heel runner like everybody else. I thought it might help. I ran on my toes for three miles, then four miles, then seven miles, and finally I could do a ten-mile run completely on my toes. I switched from high-mileage workouts to low-mileage workouts with an emphasis on quality, not quantity, because that seemed to suit me better. The high miles just wore me down. I learned to hurdle with either leg so I wouldn't have to stutter-step no matter how I approached the hurdles while running the steeplechase. That suited me, too. I experimented with a lot of things. Not everything I did worked, and I adjusted often and sometimes got frustrated. But over time, through trial and error, I found what worked best for me.

That was January of 1976. Through the winter and early spring I trained with my head down, my eyes on no one else. Without races and without looking at my teammates, I had little idea of how much I was improving. But I was getting in better shape, I was sure of that, and I was enjoying my workouts a lot more.

I set a personal goal of running fast enough that spring to qualify for the NCAA national track-and-field championships scheduled for June in Philadelphia. I didn't care what anyone else ran. I wanted to run a steeplechase race in eight minutes and fifty-five seconds, the NCAA's national meet standard. That was my goal. It was something to shoot for: Philadelphia or bust; a tangible among all the intangibles—a far off tangible, maybe, since the fastest steeplechase of my life had been run in nine minutes and twenty-five seconds three years ago when I was a freshman, but something to shoot for nonetheless.

A Real Eye-Opener

By the early part of April, after more than two months of straight training, I ran in my first steeplechase race in Tempe, Arizona, in a triangular meet with Arizona State and the University of New Mexico. As I toed the starting line, preparing to run my first competitive steeplechase in almost three years, I had high hopes, low expectations, and at least the knowledge that I'd worked hard to get here. I was off with the gun, my eyes on the track for all of the race's seven and a half laps. My determination was to run my own race and not react to what everyone else was doing. Starting slow was fine, it was part of my race strategy. My game plan was to rely on technique and a strong kick I hoped would be there for the final lap and straightaway.

When I finished and looked up at the clock I wondered if maybe I'd skipped a lap. My time was eight minutes and fifty-seven seconds. I was surprised, and my coach was in shock. I had run almost half a minute faster—a relative eternity by steeplechase standards—than any time in my life. What's more, if I could knock two seconds off that time in the next two months I could run in the national meet.

A month later I did better than that. At the Mt. SAC Relays in California, I ran eight minutes and forty-three seconds and was in the NCAAs. Two weeks after that, I ran eight minutes and forty-one seconds at the Modesto Relays and, in the process, set a new BYU school record. By early June, I found myself at Franklin Field in Philadelphia for the NCAA finals race, lined up next to the prohibitive favorite, James Munyala of UTEP, a Kenyan with world-class credentials.

I almost won that race, losing at the tape to Munyala. My time was eight minutes and twenty-seven seconds. Not only did that make me, the guy without a scholarship, an All-American (the first of five All-America awards) and the fastest American in the NCAA meet, but the officials informed me that since my time was under the eight minute and thirty-two-second qualifying standard for the Olympic Trials scheduled later that month in Eugene, Oregon, I should consider myself officially invited to try out for the United States Olympic Team that would compete that summer in the Olympic Games in Montreal.

I ran another 8:27 at the Olympic Trials in Eugene and made the first of what would be four U.S. Olympic track-and-field teams. Barely five months had expired since I had quit the track team at Brigham Young, and I was on my way to the Olympic Games.

From those first Olympic Games in Montreal in 1976 through the 1988 Olympic Games that were held in Seoul, South Korea, I competed continually on the international track-and-field circuit. During my career I accumulated the second most world-ranking points in the history of the steeplechase. And I'm convinced I never would have even begun what turned out to be a thirteen-year competitive journey if I hadn't, in my own way, stumbled onto the power of principle-driven behavior.

My New and Improved Behavior

When I changed my belief I changed my behavior—and my new behavior, unlike my previous behavior, produced results that met my needs.

My first belief was fine as long as I continued to beat other people. Basically, that was my truth—my self-worth was based on how many people I beat. If I beat the entire field, I was in good shape. If I didn't, my self-worth was in trouble. The only behavior that was acceptable was running faster than everyone else. The problem was that I couldn't control how fast everyone else was going to run, no more than I could control how hard they'd train.

It was only after I changed my belief from an external focus—beating others—to an internal focus that I was able to change my behavior. My new belief said that my self-worth was based on doing my best. I would compete only with myself. I exchanged a hindering belief that had left me with very little control for an empowering belief that left me with total control. I freed myself up so I didn't have to spend all my time worrying about others; I only had to worry about myself.

Essentially, I redefined my personal definition of winning—from beating others to getting the best out of myself. I did it by engaging the power of principle-driven behavior. At the time, I didn't articulate it that way, of course. I didn't even realize that's what I'd done. But I'd done it, nonetheless, and it changed me as a runner and a competitor. You could say it allowed me to give the proverbial 110 percent—since that's roughly how much my time improved that first year.

Besides allowing me to be the best I could be, my new belief and corresponding behavior gave me the power to be able to deal with not only the good results over that thirteen-year run, but also some results that, as far as the scoreboard was concerned, would prove to be more disappointing.

Instant Replay

Key Point

- By changing my definition of "winning," I was able to keep running and discover my personal best.

Personal Exercise

• Identify examples in your life where you made changes because your behavior wasn't working. What were the hindering and subsequent empowering beliefs behind the behaviors?

Where Do We Go from Here?

In chapter four, we'll look at pain and the key role it plays in determining what we do and when we do it.

CHAPTER FOUR

WHEN THE PAIN IS GREAT ENOUGH

We live our lives to minimize short-term pain. But the hindering beliefs that drive us are causing pain today. Why do we live with it? Because the pain of change is greater.

Knowing that my personality includes a good-sized dose of innate competitiveness—a condition no doubt exacerbated by my Texas roots—it still surprises me when I think back on my decision to walk away from the track team at BYU. I personally would have wagered that I never would have made that decision. I'd never have surrendered. I didn't think it was in my makeup. But I did. I quit, at least for a short period of time, and further reflection has brought me to the conclusion that my change was preceded by pain. When the pain got strong enough, I did something about it. I said, "Enough!"

When all else is exhausted, pain is what motivates change.

Pain doesn't have to be physical to qualify, although physical pain is the easiest to understand. Make us walk over hot coals, put us on a medieval rack, or pry our fingernails off one by one, and we'll do whatever we can to put an end to the hurting. Give us a choice between a root canal with anesthetic or without, and that's not a tough decision. What rational thinking person wants to physically hurt?

As it is with physical pain, when mental or emotional pain gets great enough, we'll also stop what we're doing. That kind of pain, despite being more difficult to quantify, can be equally intense, if not more so.

When the boss's demands get to be too much to handle, when the conflicts between family and work reach a level where no compromise is possible, when our work becomes unappreciated or so mundane we feel like screaming, when we just don't see a way out doing what we're currently doing—we'll change. When the internal pain threshold hits its limit, exactly as with physical pain, that's when we'll do anything within our power to make the pain stop. That's when we'll change.

No matter how great the cause or how strong the will, if our needs are not being met and a good deal of pain is being realized as a result, there will come a point when the alternatives will be looked at and turned to. We will eventually abandon our belief because of the pain.

There Comes a Point

This concept was most dramatically demonstrated in perhaps the most notorious battle in American history, a battle that occurred in 1863 when the Civil War had a head-on collision in Gettysburg, Pennsylvania. The Union troops had the good fortune of arriving at the battleground just ahead of the Confederate troops and, as a result, were able to lay claim to the preferred high ground. The Confederate soldiers were thus left with two choices: Stay and fight and attempt to force the Union soldiers to retreat from their strongholds or retreat back to the South from where they came. They chose to stay and fight. Despite the high probability of heavy losses, they were convinced that their cause was just (and, some believed, divine). Further, they firmly believed that their leader, General

Robert E. Lee, as beloved as any figure in military history, would not send them on a mission that was foolhardy and that they didn't have an excellent chance of winning. If he ordered them to fight, they would fight, and they were convinced they would prevail.

So it was that when Lee directed General George E. Pickett to send his troops to attack the middle of the Union line on what would turn out to be the last day of the Battle of Gettysburg, Pickett complied. With flags held high, the Confederate soldiers rushed in the direction of the Union entrenchments, storming toward the high ground of Cemetery Ridge across wide expanses of open meadows that offered little protection. The Union guns patiently waited until they came into range and then opened fire. There were nearly seven thousand Confederate casualties that day in one of the most futile military assaults ever attempted.

The courage of those Rebel troops is talked about to this day, and a monument has been erected at Gettysburg to commemorate Pickett's Charge. Despite the fact the Confederate soldiers were well intentioned and believed wholeheartedly in their cause and in their leaders, and despite their uncommon courage, it's interesting to note that there came a point when they finally stopped fighting and retreated. However dedicated and zealous and convinced that right was on their side, even they did not go to the last man. When the pain got strong enough, they stopped.

Such examples of physical conflict can help make it easier for us to visualize the relationship between beliefs and behavior. In this case the Confederate soldiers, many of whom had never been in a losing battle up to that point in the Civil War, initially behaved according to two major beliefs—one that said they were fighting for a noble and just cause that could not be denied or defeated, and one that said their leaders were infallible and therefore incapable of sending them to defeat. Those were the deeply held beliefs that sent them into battle. Those were the beliefs that drove their behavior. (And, indeed, for the first two years of the Civil

War they were beliefs that served them very well.) But the behavior was finally abandoned when it was overridden by pain. When forced by great pain and after their losses had piled up beyond human endurance, they adjusted those principles and changed their behavior.

In the final analysis, no matter how fiercely the Confederate army believed in its principles, in this case the principles acted on by the Union troops—never underestimate the value of high ground—ended up being the trump card. That was the empowering belief in this situation.

Not Even George Was That Tough

Another example is the Muhammad Ali–George Foreman fight for the heavyweight boxing championship in 1974. In boxing annals this fight is a classic and for good reason. Going into the bout, Foreman was the reigning champion, and most experts felt he would be for a good long time. A giant of a man who had followed a gold medal performance in the 1968 Olympics with a meteoric professional career, Foreman was the prohibitive favorite against Ali, the former champion who, after a number of personal troubles, was trying to mount a comeback. Foreman was younger than Ali; he was bigger, stronger, and since he was the champ, he would have to be decisively beaten if the judges were to give away his crown. Going into that fight against the aging Ali, George Foreman was the epitome of confidence and youth, a supposedly unbeatable combination that had produced knockouts over the likes of former champions Joe Frazier and Ken Norton in previous title defenses. Foreman was confident. He was convinced he could overpower any man opposite him in a boxing ring.

Then the bout began and Muhammad Ali did a curious thing. He retreated to the ropes and covered his body with his hands and arms. Foreman, seeing what he believed to be a cowering, beaten man, obliged by flailing away with lefts and rights that came with dizzying speed and fury.

As the crowd winced, Ali just stood there. For seven rounds he stayed covered up, like a lighthouse being battered by a hurricane while Foreman banged away, sure that the next blow, or the next, or the next, would drop the contender to the canvas.

An interesting transformation began to take place as the rounds wore on. Slowly but surely, Foreman's blows began to lose their sting. He was wearing out. He was running out of power. You could see it in the way he held his shoulders. As they began to droop, his punches began to slow from what had been a steady unrelenting stream to a trickle. The strong man who was absolutely sure he could batter any opponent to the mat, and particularly one who wasn't fighting back, was running out of gas.

By round eight Foreman had nothing left. And Ali had plenty. The contender took over where Foreman left off, quickly winning by a knockout with a flurry of well-placed punches against a virtually powerless opponent. When the eighth round was finished, so was Foreman. The champ had been done in by subscribing to the belief that he could defeat any opponent by overpowering him. He stuck to that belief until it became obvious—painfully obvious—that there would be nights when that just wasn't going to work, and this was one of those nights. To be sure, for the rest of a career that would be long and successful (although the Ali bout would put it on hold for a time), George Foreman changed his beliefs—and, consequently, his behavior—so he would never again be done in by the strategy Muhammad Ali called the Rope-a-Dope.

I Know How It Feels

In my own way, I can relate to George Foreman's frustration, even if I've never been knocked out by Muhammad Ali. I, too, was a professional who executed behavior that I discovered over time wasn't working.

It was called practicing law.

As I've said, I have never been accused of not being a driven person. Striving to achieve is an asset (and usually, I believe, it is an asset) that my parents ingrained into me. It's made for a busy life, particularly so during my college-age years when I did my best to balance my competitive running career with my lifelong goal of becoming a lawyer. So it was that not long after competing in the 1976 Olympic Games in Montreal, I enrolled in law school at the University of Oregon in Eugene, a track-and-field hotbed where I could be assured of never having a minute to spare as I chased my dual priorities.

After graduating from law school, I took a job with Parsons, Behle, & Latimer, one of the largest legal firms in Salt Lake City, Utah. The firm put my name on its letterhead, gave me a wood-paneled office with a view, a secretary, a staff of paralegals, my personal code number for the copy machine, and directions to the library. In five years, if I kept up my billable hours and handled my caseload satisfactorily, I could be a partner. Five years after that I could potentially be a senior partner. I was on my way.

At first I was enthusiastic. As I said, entering the law had been a lifelong goal of mine. My father was a lawyer and so was my grandfather (whom I was named after) as well as my great grandfather. I thought practicing law was what I was supposed to do, what I was cut out to do. It was the cloth I was made of. I thought I had the genes for it.

Besides that, and perhaps even more important, during my growing-up years I had been strongly influenced to become a lawyer because of the prestige that I perceived was associated with the profession. All my childhood inputs were that the law was a good profession and that lawyers were important. When people would ask me, "What's your name and what do you do?" my belief was that by saying, "I'm a lawyer," I would be important. In other words, my belief was that I'd only be as important and good as my profession and as others perceived the importance of that profession. A wholehearted belief in that personal truth made my decision to do what it took to graduate from law school and join a prestigious law firm an easy one.

But the more I practiced law, the more I noticed a behavior pattern that was disturbing to me. Before long, every Wednesday became "hump day" for me. All I thought about during the early part of the week was how much I wanted to get over hump day and head for the weekend. Every Friday for me was T.G.I.F.—Thank Goodness It's Friday. I wanted the week to be over because I enjoyed what I did on the weekends a lot more than what I did during the week. As a result, the weekends flew by. I became a member of the weekday clock-watcher club, Monday through Friday.

Still, I persisted at my chosen profession for a number of what I maintained (and still maintain to this day) were very good reasons. Money was one of them, and the prestige I felt I enjoyed because of what I was doing was another. I wanted my father to approve of me, of course, and there were many other factors. As time wore on, and as the pain of practicing law became greater and greater for me—a pain that came from my needs not being satisfied—I started to reassess my reasons for being a lawyer. I rethought my personal truths.

The Light Came On

I began to think that maybe the most important thing about your profession isn't what other people think of you. The most important thing just might be to feel fulfilled and enjoy the day-to-day practice of your chosen profession. The law is a terrific profession if you're suited for it, like my father or, say, Clarence Darrow or Racehorse Haynes. But was I suited for it? I wondered. My personality thrives on being with people and on variety. I noticed that writing memos in the law office and doing research in the library didn't enthuse me like it did many of my colleagues. Preparing for trial didn't excite me as much as preparing for, say, a race on the track or one of my many opportunities to speak to groups about my Olympic experiences. Keeping billable hours and being in a fixed-time circumstance was stifling to me. The structure was constricting. A lot of people thrive on eight to five schedules, but I don't.

I may travel and work fourteen-hour days, but it doesn't seem like it if I'm going somewhere and I'm not tied to a clock.

Over time, all of this became increasingly clear to me. As a result, my beliefs began to change. When the pain of practicing law became greater than the benefit of being able to tell people I practiced law, I altered my beliefs. My old belief was that my self-worth was based on how I perceived others viewed my profession. My new belief was that my self-worth was based on how much I enjoyed my profession. I didn't execute this "replacing of beliefs" any more consciously in this instance than when I altered my beliefs as a college runner nearly ten years earlier. Then, as now, I reacted to the pain I was feeling, and that's what effected the change of beliefs.

A Lifetime Leave

Acting on my new belief, in 1984 I took a leave of absence from Parsons, Behle, & Latimer. I've been on that leave of absence ever since. I was determined to live by my new belief and to have my behavior reflect that new belief. As I left the firm, I was determined to feel fulfilled by my profession, even if I wasn't sure what it would be. I worked as a sportscaster for a period of time, and I started my own company called Athletes Unlimited. I was doing these things trying to find what really worked for me. I was actively seeking. Then I ran across the Franklin Quest Company in 1987. For over ten years, I worked with Franklin Quest as a curriculum developer and motivational trainer. That worked for me. I was happy to stay.

Not long after I started working for Franklin, I realized what I'd been missing: There were no more hump days or T.G.I.F.'s. It didn't matter anymore what day of the week it was. I looked forward to Mondays as much as I looked forward to Saturdays. I felt satisfaction, enjoyment, and peace with what I was doing. The difference was tremendous. I had changed. The pain was gone.

Still, it was not an easy change. Replacing beliefs is rarely easy. When I left the legal profession, I really struggled personally because I was changing beliefs that had been part of me practically my entire life. I wondered if my dad thought less of me than of my two brothers who were still practicing attorneys. I wondered if society would now perceive of me as less of a person if I wasn't practicing law. I wondered what the other attorneys thought. I really struggled with that. When I first started working with Franklin and people asked me what I did, I'd answer them with, "I'm an attorney; I work with Franklin." I answered that way because I was still tied into the belief that what people really thought of you was tied into what they thought of your profession (and besides, technically it was true, I was still an attorney). If I said I was an attorney, I'd be well thought of. So I'd answer, "I'm an attorney; I work with Franklin." It took me a year and a half to overcome that—a year and a half of living the new principle before it became stronger and more persuasive than the old one—and I could say simply, "I work with Franklin."

After I left the law, I remember visiting Dallas, where my brother Will lived. I was passing through town, and I called him one evening and his wife answered. I said, "Is Will there?" and she said, "No, he's been working late every night on a big case." I remember thinking, "Gee, I'm glad I'm not doing that." I'm sure it was fine and satisfying for Will but it wouldn't have been fine for me. It wasn't that I wasn't working just as many hours. If you counted the nights away from home, I was actually working more hours than I had as a lawyer. But I wasn't counting the hours anymore, and that made a huge difference.

I reached yet another point in my professional career when the pain was great enough to inspire me to yet another career change. I say, "pain," but the truth is that I was happy—as I already said—at Franklin Covey. But I recognized that while my new principle was working, there was a better principle that I could be living by (we'll talk about more empowering beliefs in chapter fifteen). I had adjusted my thinking when I changed my career path and joined Franklin Covey. My thinking then went to the next level—I wanted to know how I could make a difference in the lives of as many people as possible. The answer was to start my own company. My new belief of changing lives led to my partnering with the other founders of MonaVie to found a new company. Had my principles never changed, I would still be trudging through my daily grind as an unhappy attorney. Instead, because the pain was great enough, I made the change, and my life is better because of it.

What Dad Thought

Not long after my visit to Dallas, I was working with the space people at NASA, presenting a seminar, and I told them my story about my legal career. They asked me what my dad thought about my leaving the legal profession. I said I'd never asked him. They said, ask him and report back. So I called Dad up that weekend and I said, "Dad, NASA wants to know what you thought about my leaving the legal profession." You know what he said? He said, "Henry, when you left the legal profession, I thought you'd thrown away your education." But then he added something that was very interesting to me. He said, "But I see now that you're probably doing more good for others than if you were practicing law."

I don't know if my dad just thought I was a bad attorney or what (and I didn't press the issue), but I came to realize through our talk that he wasn't a lawyer because others would think highly of him, and he'd never viewed me as a lawyer in that context either. The personal truths that had guided him and kept him in his chosen profession were different from the personal truths that had guided me to mine. He was a lawyer first and foremost to help other people. You don't tell my dad attorney jokes. He's really offended by them. To him, the law is a service profession. That's how he sees himself as a lawyer, and that's how he saw me as a lawyer. If I wasn't going to serve others by practicing law, it pleased him that I could serve others in another, perhaps even better, way.

What's pleased me—and him—is that I found a profession that's enabled me to feel a sense of self-worth based on my own personal enthusiasm and enjoyment of that profession, and not on how I believe others perceive that profession. When I changed the belief that drove my behavior, I changed professions. It was that simple. Just as back in college I became a different runner when I changed my beliefs, I became a different professional when I changed my occupational beliefs from without to within.

The Pain Made Me Do It

In both cases, nothing would have happened if pain, in one or another of its many forms, hadn't ultimately gotten my attention. The pain in each case was different. The pain I felt as a runner was the pain of frustration of not getting where I wanted to go. I liked to run; I just didn't care for how it was making me feel. As a lawyer, the pain I felt wasn't out of frustration. To the contrary, I was prospering nicely as a barrister. I was making reasonably good money and was generally well thought of in my firm. Professionally, I seemed to be cutting it. The pain I was feeling was out of dissatisfaction. I wasn't doing what suited my makeup, and I knew it.

Once the pain was great enough in both instances, I was motivated to make the necessary changes in beliefs to drive my behavior in new directions. In hindsight I can see that clearly now, and in my work I've been able to better understand the laws of cause and effect that were at work in my life, even when I didn't know they were. More importantly, I have been able to appreciate that it isn't necessary to see how much pain we can withstand before it's possible to change the hindering beliefs that drive the behaviors that cause that pain. You don't need to do it my way. My way was the hard way. A clear understanding of the dynamics of principle-driven behavior can help us make corrections before the pain surfaces, let alone becomes intolerable.

Suffering is not a requirement, and while it's true that no one's life can be guaranteed to be free of discomfort all the time, it's also true that through the power of belief-driven behavior, casualties can be kept to a low minimum.

The best part is the choice is all ours, and it applies to all of our various situations. If something isn't working in our lives, and we're not sure why, a look at the belief that's driving our behavior can open vistas we've never seen before.

Instant Replay

Key Points

- When our needs are not being met, the result is pain.

- When the pain gets strong enough, we'll change.

- The pain doesn't have to get that strong. By getting in touch with our beliefs, we can effect change that will considerably cut down on the suffering.

Personal Exercise

- Make a list of recurrent situations in your life that cause pain (emotional as well as physical). Identify possible beliefs that are causing the pain and which needs are not being met.

Where Do We Go from Here?

In chapter five, we'll look at the very real physiological problems that are the direct result of hindering beliefs, and ways to avoid them.

CHAPTER FIVE

DISEASES OF CHOICE

In the process of minimizing pain today, we form addictions. These addictions help us hide from our pain and ignore the need to create new beliefs that can get rid of the pain for good.

Right now you may be thinking, well, you'd have to be crazy not to want to avoid all that pain. Who wouldn't want to change beliefs that are hindering? But wanting to and pulling it off aren't the same thing. It's one thing to know you have what you need to storm the beach; it's another to actually storm the beach. The reason can be summed up in one word: obstacles.

Every day, all kinds of obstacles regularly appear in our path. Their existence is a given; they're a part of life, and many of them are so constant, they're like clockwork. We can count on them. It's why I've always paralleled running the steeplechase with running the race of life. In both cases, just when you really get cruising, a hurdle appears. However, the steeplechase is easier than life. At least in the steeplechase you know the obstacles are coming and that they're going to be in the same spot every time. That makes it a lot easier to prepare.

In life, there's no way of knowing what's coming next, or when. Think of it: billions of Belief Lenses, all of them different, coming together every second of every day as we interrelate with one another.

That can be an exciting thought, or it can make you not want to get out of bed in the morning. It depends on how you look at it. My approach to running the steeplechase taught me that. When I focused on everyone else in the race and worried about what they were going to do, the races weren't nearly as enticing and enjoyable to me as when I focused on how I was going to run the race and what I was going to do. That change in belief gave me an entirely different perspective on the exact same race. Everything was less imposing, obstacles included, when I focused only on those things I could personally manage.

Control What We Can

More than two hundred years ago, Benjamin Franklin was driven by the same realization. I think he articulated a Natural Law perfectly when he said:

While we may not be able to control all that happens to us, we can control what happens inside us.

That's the key: knowing what we can control (ourselves) and doing something about it. We can make our own choices. We get to choose how we react to all that happens to us.

Realizing the enormity of those things that can happen to us can be helpful in preparing for our reactions to them. If we sit down and make a list of the obstacles and hurdles present in our lives, it won't be long before the list is running off the end of the paper. A typical obstacles list for most of us would include such things as finances, family, workload, boss, traffic, relationships, deadlines, coworkers, mergers, change, and unreal expectations.

To our long list of obstacles we can add a second list, this one consisting of symptoms that are the result of those obstacles. This list will typically go off the page, too, including such symptoms as headaches, high blood pressure, ulcers, depression, anxiety, anger, nervousness, fatigue, twitching eyes, insomnia, illness, overeating, irritability, helplessness, an overwhelmed feeling, and perhaps of most significance, a barrage of negative self-talk. Notice these symptoms are physical, emotional, and mental in nature. They run the whole spectrum.

Obstacles Aren't Symptoms, and Vice Versa

Sometimes we confuse the symptoms with the obstacles. That's easy to do. How often do we hear people say, for example, that high blood pressure is their problem when the reality is that it's their belief or perception about their demanding boss or their overbearing workload that is actually the source of their discontent and the cause of their high blood pressure? The boss is the obstacle. The high blood pressure is the symptom.

One of the saddest of our modern symptom diseases is anorexia nervosa. Medically speaking, anorexia nervosa is described as a psychosomatic disorder typified by self-starvation, which occurs most commonly among adolescent females.

Although this disorder was not as prevalent or as well known thirty years ago, it's now estimated that as many as 1 percent of young women in the United States are afflicted with anorexia nervosa. Ten percent of those who contract the disorder die because of it. Yet it is based primarily on a psychological perception the afflicted person has that she is much fatter than she really is.

This condition, the medical literature suggests, typically develops in connection with one or more of the following: a sudden move or change of environment, mental depression, peer pressure, and dysfunctional family life. As with high blood pressure, ulcers, the eating disorder bulimia (a purging disease that often goes hand in hand with anorexia nervosa), or any of the other ailments increasing in incidence in modern society, anorexia nervosa seems to qualify as a symptom. Like the others, it seems to owe its existence to the mental obstacles that bring it on.

Stress Is a Perception

A popular modern label for these obstacles and their symptoms is stress. What, really, is stress? Let me offer this definition: Stress is simply our response to events we perceive as threatening to our needs. That's an important definition to remember, and it holds a key distinction. Stress is a response to what we perceive. It's our reaction. We own it. Whenever we perceive a threat to one of our four basic needs, we will respond mentally, emotionally, and physically. Our response is what stress is all about. Stress is a response based upon a perception of a threat.

Statistics from the pain medication business paint a picture of modern stress that suggests its enormity and gives us insight into just how strongly we respond to what we see as our modern obstacles, or stressors.

In America in 2010 alone, the over-the-counter pain medication industry sold more than $17 billion worth of products (The Nielsen Company, 2011). That's how much Americans spend for nonprescription remedies to treat aches and pains, and that's not counting prescription drugs prescribed by doctors for more serious symptoms such as depression, high blood pressure, ulcers, and high cholesterol—what's more, that amount doesn't even include Wal-Mart! Literally tens of millions of prescriptions are filled every year for these conditions. Drugs such as Prozac (used to treat depression) have become household names.

These conditions are costing corporate America billions of dollars every year. It is estimated that it costs corporations over $4,000 annually per employee for health care, and 75 percent of those costs are for so-called stress-related symptoms.

You Only Catch Them from Yourself

Now comes the multibillion-dollar question: How much control do we have over these symptoms?

The answer: nearly total control.

Except for certain genetic situations and bacterial-induced ulcers over which we obviously have no control and for which the above-mentioned drugs serve a valuable function, these are diseases of choice. They are self-induced. They are not contagious. You can't go home from work and say, "Dear, I shook hands with the boss today and picked up high blood pressure." Or, "Dear, I shook hands with a coworker today and picked up depression." A friend doesn't shake hands with you and pass on one of these symptoms. We give them to ourselves. Yet it's these symptoms that account for the majority of health and pain problems. That's right, the majority! They even make it much easier for us to catch bacteria and viruses that have nothing to do with the symptoms on our lists. They merely make us weak and more susceptible.

That's the bad news.

And also the good news.

If we can choose to have these symptoms, we can choose not to have them.

Let's take a look at traffic. Traffic is a good example, I think, because it's probably fair to assume that all of us have experienced some grief due to traffic hassles. It's a universal complaint, an across-the-board aggravation. Getting stuck in traffic, no matter how short the duration, no matter what kind of vehicle we're driving, is a waste of time; it keeps us from being productive or from getting to a meeting or home in time for dinner. Dealing with other drivers is a pain, and road construction annoys us. Our tendency is to look at traffic as a necessary evil, sometimes even as a foe.

Let's change the setup. Let's say the next time you're in a traffic jam, I will pay you one thousand dollars for every minute you're stuck in traffic. How will you respond? Of course the next time you're stuck in traffic, you'll love it! You'll be courteous. You'll let everyone go ahead of you. You'll go out of your way to find problem roads. You won't care if you never get home.

Now, notice that the traffic did not change. It was the exact same event. What changed was your perception of that event. We took something we perceived as threatening, annoying, and challenging, changed the scenario, and turned it into something we could actually look forward to. It was all based on perception. That's all we changed—nothing more, nothing less. The traffic conditions weren't altered a bit. Instead of being uptight, anxious, and angry, we were able to replace that with enthusiasm and excitement.

It's How We Choose to Look at It

Events, then, are not the problem. Perception is the problem. Attitude is the problem. How we choose to look at it is the problem. I like the story about the man standing in line to get his driver's license. After he arrives at the Department of Motor Vehicles, he has to stand in the requisite multiple lines—standard procedure when your driver's license comes up for renewal.

But the more lines he stands in, the more agitated and anxious he becomes. His patience dwindles. He can't believe the time he's wasting. All the while, however, he can't help but notice that the lady in front of him seems totally nonplussed by the whole ridiculous time-consuming process. She's in a great mood. Line after line, hour after hour, she continues to smile. Obviously, she's enjoying the whole experience. Finally, by the last line, he just has to ask her: "This is really stressing me out, all these lines," he says, "and you're so happy. I've got to know why."

The lady answers, "Oh, I'm a professional line waiter. I'm being paid by someone to stand in line for them."

Remember, stress is how we respond to events based upon our perceptions. The problem for many of us today is that the way we're responding is killing us.

That is not an idle statement. It's not meant merely for shock value. Sadly, our responses often are killing us in a very real sense. A physiological understanding of exactly what happens when we create stress by our responses can be very instructive.

Introducing Ugh

First, let me introduce an old friend we'll call Ugh (see adjoining illustration). Notice that Ugh is making the acquaintance of a saber-toothed tiger. The tiger is Ugh's Stone-Age obstacle, and Ugh is exhibiting a Stone-Age response. Remember, our definition of stress is that it's a response to anything we perceive as threatening to our needs. Ugh perceives—and we have no problem assuming rightfully so—that the saber-toothed tiger is threatening his need to live.

The tiger represents a sudden threat and that triggers what we call an alarm response. That alarm response in turn sets into action an amazing number of physiological changes in his body. As soon as he sees the tiger (and simultaneously perceives the threat), Ugh's adrenal gland secretes a hormone we're all familiar with called adrenaline. Adrenaline, in turn, triggers chemical reactions in Ugh's body that empower him to run faster or fight harder, whichever he chooses, in order to hopefully survive the threat to his life. Very quickly, all kinds of things happen as adrenaline is sent through Ugh's body. For one thing, his blood pressure increases so his blood will move faster and get to Ugh's major muscle groups, which will be required for some major work whether his decision is to fight or to flee. As Ugh's heart beats faster, causing a rise in his blood pressure, and as the blood rushes to his major muscles, the circulation in Ugh's hands and feet slows down and his hands and feet, as a result, get cool. He doesn't need blood in his hands or feet right now; he needs it in his muscles, at the core of his body, and that's what his brain is telling his heart. Send the blood where it belongs. Now!

Meanwhile, as Ugh's blood pressure is rising, sugars and fats are being rushed into the blood stream. This is so Ugh will have plenty of fuel for his muscles. He'll have a sudden burst of energy when he needs it; he'll have power. As the sugars and fats rush to the muscles, his digestion becomes acidic because the blood is leaving the stomach, again for the major muscles, and what's left in the stomach are the acids and juices. These acids and juices will produce what Ugh will later describe as a knot in his stomach. Like his cold hands and feet, the knot in his stomach is an indication that he is responding to a sudden threat and he is in an alarm response. At the moment, it's not a bad sign; it's a very good sign, in fact. A sign that all battle stations are ready. The hands, the feet, and the stomach—they're all sacrificing for the cause.

The thickness of Ugh's blood changes, too. Blood platelets are sent to the blood stream to thicken the blood in case the tiger bites him. Thick blood clots faster and makes it harder to bleed to death. Other changes occur simultaneously. Ugh's hearing becomes more acute (the better to hear the tiger) and his eyes dilate (the better to see the tiger). Everything he needs to physically survive—to fight or to flee—is put in place because his life is on the line, and these are the natural physiological responses.

So that's the alarm response, and in this case, and for Ugh's sake, let's say it worked. Ugh sees the tiger in time and uses his sudden burst of energy to smack the tiger with his club, and then he runs back to his cave where he rolls a huge rock over the opening. Safe to live another day!

The Alarm Response

Now it's the next day, and while searching for food to satisfy his need to live, Ugh is walking down the same path where he encountered the tiger the day before.

What's Ugh saying to himself? It's not hard to imagine him repeating to himself, "Where's the tiger? Where's the tiger?" Ugh is going to be anything but nonchalant and casual. He's ready. Any movement in the brush, he's there. Any little thing, he's prepared. He's in what is called a vigilant state, and his body is already into a vigilant response.

There's a difference between the alarm response Ugh had yesterday and the vigilant response he's now experiencing. The alarm response called for action; the vigilant response calls for preparation in case action is needed. As Ugh walks down the path, he is heavy into preparation.

To prepare for another possible tiger encounter, the adrenal gland doesn't produce adrenaline as it would for an actual attack, but instead releases a hormone called cortisol. Like its cousin adrenaline, cortisol triggers a number of chemical reactions in Ugh's body, some of them similar to those caused by adrenaline and some not so similar. Cortisol is the hormone of preparation. One of the things it can do is trigger the liver to increase its production of cholesterol. While cholesterol is looked at mainly today as a menace to society, it definitely has its beneficial purposes, primarily as a repair agent. The same stickiness property that causes cholesterol to clog arteries also allows it to line and repair cells—a most useful property in Ugh's body if he's going to have to battle that tiger again today. He's bound to damage some cells, and extra cholesterol is already in store to help him if that happens. Another useful purpose of cholesterol is to lubricate and pad the joints, something Ugh will also need in the event of an encounter with the tiger.

It's also educational to note that the two forms of cholesterol (HDL = good cholesterol, LDL = bad cholesterol) also relate to Ugh. Survival responses trigger the sticky bad cholesterol (LDL) to repair cells. And what's the biggest factor in raising good cholesterol (HDL), which binds to carry away the bad cholesterol? You guessed it: physical exertion— exactly what Ugh does when he fights or runs from the tiger.

Cortisol also triggers the body to retain fluids. If Ugh is going to fight or flee, he'll need to sweat more so that his body temperature will remain cool. Cortisol helps take care of that. Similarly, body fat stores go up, and Ugh, in this preparation stage, will have a craving for sugars and fats. If it's fight or flight, those sources of fuel will need to be on hand. Also, cortisol triggers Ugh's immune system to shut down. Now you may ask yourself, why on earth would his immune system shut down? The answer is that it's his immune system that constantly requires the most energy, and at the moment Ugh doesn't need his immune system nearly as much as he needs all available energy to either fight harder or run faster. He isn't worried about getting sick, not at this moment. He's worried about living. So the immune system shuts down, temporarily, so the energy it usually uses can become a part of the survival response. If the tiger comes around the bend, Ugh is as ready as he'll ever be.

The Cost Is Toxic

There is a price to pay for all this preparedness, however, and that price is in the form of toxins or poisons. Every time the body has a chemical reaction there is a byproduct, or a toxin, that's released. Just as in a nuclear reaction there is radioactivity or fallout, in the same manner, whenever your body triggers chemical reactions, there's a toxin that is released as a result. To facilitate his primitive survival responses—either alarm or vigilance—Ugh would have up to 1,400 chemical reactions, and he would have a fairly equivalent amount of resultant toxins released into his bloodstream. When Ugh fights or runs, these toxins are no problem; they're either burned up or sweated out of the body. During the first twelve minutes of physical exertion, the body burns exclusively what's in the blood stream. So when Ugh physically exerts, he's burning toxins. As he sweats, he purges more toxins. Thus Ugh dissipates the poison. He gets rid of the toxic byproducts of adrenaline and cortisol.

Now I'm going to deliver some good news and bad news as we bring the example of Ugh into the present day.

The good news is that the same adrenaline and cortisol reactions experienced by Ugh are still available today. Like Stone-Age Ugh, each of us has the Incredible Hulk inside. Have you ever read about a woman lifting a car to save a child? How did she do it? Adrenaline! That power has not been lost over the centuries. We still use adrenaline and cortisol on a regular basis.

The bad news is that when we get upset over a soda machine swallowing our dollar bill, our blood thickens in case the soda machine bites us.

Introducing Doug

Look at the picture of Doug, the modern-day Ugh (see illustration). Just as Ugh fought the saber-toothed tiger, Doug fights the soda machine. Whereas Ugh's battles centered on physical threats, Doug's center mostly on mental threats.

Doug wants a soda. He puts in his money. But this machine hasn't come through for Doug before, and he's not entirely sure what to expect. As he pushes the button for the soda of his choice, he's already braced for a confrontation—a confrontation with an inanimate machine!

At this point, Doug's body is responding exactly as Ugh's body responded when Ugh came down the path wondering if the tiger was going to be there. It's going into a vigilant response. The adrenal gland is producing cortisol, the liver is increasing its production of cholesterol, the cortisol is ordering the body to retain fluids and to shut down its immune system, and all of the resultant chemical reactions are releasing thousands of toxins into his system. Toxins that ultimately will have nowhere to go. Why will they have nowhere to go? Because Doug's fight with the soda machine is mental—the machine cannot hurt him physically.

For the most part, our modern lives revolve around mental obstacles and threats, not physical obstacles and threats. Not many of our threats have a lot to do with physical survival anymore; they're not driven by the need to live. We don't run into many saber-toothed tigers. But the body doesn't know the difference.

Whether the perceived threat is mental or physical, the body will respond with adrenaline and cortisol. Anytime there is the perception of a threat (remember, that's our definition of stress), our cholesterol is going to go up, we'll retain fats and sugars, our immune systems will shut down, our digestion will become acidic, and toxins will flood the body. But today, whenever we have a mental threat, what do we do with the toxins? Do we fight or flee? The answer is almost never. We may mentally exert, but we rarely physically exert. The result? Too often we are left to literally stew in our juices.

If you've ever cooked stew, have you noticed how the meat in the stew deteriorates and falls apart as the juices around it break it down? Well, these mental threats cause what I call, "heart stew." When toxins are allowed to go unchecked in the body, the same thing happens to our hearts that happens to the meat in stew. Left to accumulate in the heart muscle tissue, toxins will break down the heart muscle and form what's called a "contraction band lesion." The contraction band is that band of muscle that makes your heart contract. When toxins are left lingering in the heart muscle, a lesion develops and the heart is seriously weakened.

Silent Killers

Contraction band lesions are by no means the only complications of modern-day mental threats, but they are representative of the many forms of silent killers that are at work in our modern society. Statistics indicate that contraction band lesions are found in 86 percent of the approximately 400,000 sudden deaths annually reported in the United States. This isn't a minor symptom. This is no small problem. Its prevalence is staggering. Probably the most disturbing part is that our modern-day heart testing systems aren't designed to detect the problem. They're set up to test us physically, not mentally.

Think about it. How do doctors test us today to see how we're responding physically to our mental threats? They'll put us on a treadmill or a heart-rate monitor, or they'll measure our EKG and our oxygen intake capacity, or test our blood pressure. Let's say you go in and get your blood pressure tested and the doctor says, "Your blood pressure's great; get out of here." That afternoon you die of a heart attack. Why didn't the doctor pick it up? Maybe it's because you like your doctor; you're relaxed in his or her office, and you think your doctor's a great doctor. So your doctor is not something you consider to be an obstacle or a threat, and your blood pressure is fine in the office. It's a chance for you to relax from the pressures of your busy schedule.

The point is it isn't easy to physically test to see if we're building toxins to a dangerous level in our bodies. The only way I could accurately test your blood pressure as it relates to anxiety and stress is if I hooked you up to a blood pressure cuff for twenty-four hours and profiled what your blood pressure did all day long. Different situations trigger different results, as do different times of the year. There have been studies, for example, that show a CPA's cholesterol level going up by as much as 100 points during tax season, and then going back down again when the returns have all been mailed off to the IRS.

It's important to know if we're accumulating toxins. If we're constantly going into a vigilant response and rarely, if ever, entering the action-response phase, that's plain unhealthy! We're the human equivalent of a fireplace with the chimney closed. Bear in mind that we are not talking about doing away with adrenaline and cortisol. To the contrary. Those two natural hormones are valuable in our lives. In some of our occupations and recreational pursuits, it's imperative that they are present to help us perform better.

What we are talking about is finding a way to better balance our stress response. Our overloaded stress levels, as we've been discussing, create myriad other problems in our body. We've discussed the buildup of toxins in our systems, but we haven't touched on some of the other problems that affect our health. Dr. Shawn Talbott, a leading expert on biochemistry and stress, has created an insightful book, which he titled *The Secret of Vigor*. In this book, Dr. Talbott notes that our modern, stressful lifestyles not only elevate stress hormone levels, which impair the functioning of other hormones like testosterone and insulin, they also imbalance our blood sugar levels, increase inflammation, and exacerbate the damage caused by oxidative stress.

One of the responses that both Ugh and Doug experienced was an increase in the amount of sugar in their blood. Have you ever noticed that when you are feeling stressed, you have increased cravings for sweet treats? This is a natural response to stress. Your body recognizes a need for the quick energy that sugar provides. Unfortunately, we do not burn off that extra stress, causing it to be stored—most often as fat in the abdominal region. Aside from not being all that attractive, fat around the midsection has been tied to cardiovascular disease and other health issues.

In an interesting twist, Dr. Talbott notes that all that extra sugar actually causes an increase in AGEs (Advanced Glycation End products). These AGEs cause an increase in inflammation. Inflammation is another natural way that your body responds to injury in order to protect itself. But, as with most things, too much or sustained inflammation leads to other problems.

What about oxidative stress? Your body is under constant attack from free radicals. Free radicals occur naturally in the environment and in your body, and your body has a natural response to these oxidizing agents. But when all the pollutants and toxins from our modern world are coupled with the toxins created by our stressed-out lives, and then compounded by a body already overwhelmed by other issues, oxidative stress really begins to take its toll.

Are you beginning to see a pattern here? As Dr. Talbott notes in his work, all of these issues are interrelated. When one issue is out of balance, it has a negative effect on the other areas as well. So, if you don't have enough antioxidants in your system to battle oxidative stress, chances are you will have too much inflammation and your blood sugar will also be out of balance. And, as a result, your stress hormone levels—adrenaline and cortisol—are going to be elevated as well. Pretty soon, you're caught in a downward-spiraling vortex that perpetuates itself.

Know What's Going On

It's important to know what is going on with our bodies. When we know that our stress hormone levels are too high, our blood sugar is out of balance, our body's inflammatory response is in overdrive, or our body is succumbing to oxidative stress, then we can do something about it. But how do you know?

Fortunately, because all of these issues are interrelated, logic dictates that by knowing the status of one, we can safely surmise what the other areas are doing. In other words, if we know that our blood sugar levels are out of whack, we can assume that our antioxidant levels are also suffering. So, what am I suggesting here? That you should go in for weekly blood tests to see what your hormone levels are or invest in your own blood sugar meter? Not necessarily. There is a better way.

Science has developed a fast, thorough, non-invasive way to test one of the areas of health we've been discussing—oxidative stress—and I'm proud to say that MonaVie provides it. The MonaVie VIEW Antioxidant Scanner uses pressure-mediated reflection spectroscopy to test your body's antioxidant levels. When you insert your finger into the scanner, it is lightly squeezed and then scanned with a harmless light, and, within 60 seconds, you will know what your antioxidant levels are. Knowing what your antioxidant levels are will tell you if you are protecting your body sufficiently from oxidative stress. If your score is high, most likely your blood sugar levels, inflammation, and stress hormones levels are doing alright as well. But if your score is low, then you've got some work to do.

Another area that we can work on to improve our stress levels and response is to learn to better control how and when to release adrenaline and cortisol. It's important to know what's going on with the adrenaline and cortisol we have at our disposal so we can use them effectively and take care to rid ourselves of the resultant toxins. If we are constantly triggering adrenaline and cortisol in reaction to mental obstacles only, and we aren't physically exerting to reduce the buildup of toxicity, then we're in trouble (whether we know it or not), and we need to do something about it.

That doesn't mean that if the boss gets my blood pressure up first thing in the morning that I go to the boss and say, "Boss, you're stressing me out and I've got toxins, so I've got to go physically exert. I've got to release them. I'll be back in a minute." The procedure doesn't have to be that immediate. It's like with a tooth. If you eat food and leave it unchecked in your teeth for twenty-four hours it turns to plaque and starts the decaying process. Does that mean you'll have a cavity the next day or the day after that? No. It takes a while to decay a tooth. It's the same way with the heart muscle. It won't decay overnight. If we go three or four days building up toxins and don't physically exert, that doesn't necessarily mean we're going to get a contraction band lesion. But we're going to be in trouble if we let it go unchecked indefinitely. If we're aware of the possible toxicity levels going on inside our bodies and have some kind of consistent physical exertion to counteract that, we can do like Ugh and get rid of the poisons. We can avoid the deadly combination of a pressurized workload and no physical exertion.

Biopsy or Autopsy

I get asked a lot if it's possible to detect a contraction band lesion. I say yes, there are two ways: with a biopsy or an autopsy! The next question I get asked is if it's possible to get rid of, or repair, a contraction band lesion that already exists. The answer, unfortunately, is no. Whenever we damage muscle tissue, we form scar tissue and we cannot get rid of scar tissue. That doesn't mean we're left without remedies. Through exercise we can build healthy tissue around the scar tissue already formed. We can always strengthen that which has been weakened, even if we can't go back and start over.

As we leave Ugh and Doug, we find that we're basically left with two choices. Either we do away with adrenaline and cortisol, or we physically exert to eliminate the harmful toxins and the potentially dangerous physical conditions, such as contraction band lesions, that adrenaline and cortisol are capable of producing. Those are our choices, and it should be obvious which choice is in our best interest.

For those of us who have jobs where adrenaline helps us perform better, an exercise schedule is critical. The same thing that was true for Ugh's body is true for our bodies: We were made to move. We're meant to physically exert.

Another option is to help our bodies balance their stress levels. Once again, let's consult an expert. Dr. Talbott recommends the use of supplements that help your body to bring stress hormone levels into balance again. Working with Dr. Talbott, MonaVie has developed Vset—a stress-busting formulation that promotes relaxation and rejuvenation. Vset consists of a morning and evening pill that help you to maintain an even keel in the modern world's turbulent waters.

We can literally save our lives by understanding what's going on inside of us—and doing something about it—as we deal with modern-day mental obstacles that we perceive as threats. We can see modern-day saber-toothed tigers all around us in our workplaces today. The soda machine is not alone as a potential stressor.

Awareness is the key to the cure, just as awareness is the key to recognizing that, unlike saber-toothed tigers, our modern-day obstacles and threats are in large measure defined by us. We're luckier than Ugh. The saber-toothed tiger was a saber-toothed tiger with real saber teeth no matter what he thought. He couldn't wish it away. He couldn't get rid of the problem by changing his perception. But we can wish many of our threats away. In our modern mental experiences, we can create saber-toothed tigers or we can eliminate saber-toothed tigers. They can come with or without teeth—all according to our perceptions, which are a result of our beliefs. When we put empowering beliefs in place, the result will be an elimination of many of our "tigers."

Instant Replay

Key Points

- Diseases of stress are diseases of choice.

- We can't always control what happens to us, but we can control what happens inside us.

- Stress is how we respond to events based upon our perception.

- Our bodies are meant to move. That's how we release toxins. Good health depends on it.

Personal Exercise

- Take an inventory of the times you missed work or took prescription drugs during the past year. Was the root cause a contagious disease or a disease of choice?

Where Do We Go from Here?

In chapter six, we'll look at warning lights that, if heeded, can prevent diseases of choice and, if ignored, can lead to addictions that cater to these diseases.

CHAPTER SIX

DON'T SACRIFICE WHAT YOU WANT MOST FOR WHAT YOU WANT NOW

Take it from an old distance runner: it's the long run that matters.

As a runner, I've developed a keen appreciation for endurance. I admire stamina and a strong will. That's probably why one of my favorite characters in literature is the old fisherman in Ernest Hemingway's classic book, *The Old Man and the Sea*. Hemingway doesn't tell us much background about the old man, only that his name is Santiago and he's a fisherman who's spent his days working the waters off the Cuban coastline. We get to know the old man well as he hooks a giant fish, a catch of a lifetime, and holds on as days turn into nights and back into days again. It's really too much for the old man, this ordeal, but he won't cut the line because all his life he's been in search of a great fish like this. Whenever the pain and the fatigue seem to be unbearable, the old man has some terrific talks with himself that are the real essence of the book:

It was a great temptation to rest in the bow and let the fish make one circle by himself without recovering any line. But when the strain showed the fish had turned to come toward the boat, the old man rose to his feet and started the pivoting and the weaving pulling that brought in all the line he gained.

I'm tireder than I have ever been, he thought, and now the trade wind is rising. But that will be good to take him in with. I need that badly.

He does not let go. The old man knew what he wanted and refused to give up so he could be more comfortable for the moment. Talk about self-help! No one else was there to do it for him, so he talked himself into it.

Think Long-Term

It may be an extreme example, and one that's far from the waters we might fish in, but it has some definite parallels to the concept of belief-driven behavior and the forces of fatigue that try to short-circuit our attempts to achieve our personal best. The old man's beliefs were firmly in place, and he wasn't about to deviate from them. What he wanted most was to be a great fisherman, and landing this great fish would validate that; it was a course he would not turn from, even if it meant being dragged bleeding and broken halfway to Venezuela. He would not sacrifice what he wanted most for what he wanted now.

That's a Natural Law we would all do well to commit to memory:

Don't sacrifice what you want most for what you want now.

Just as the old man knew that by hanging on to the fish, he would, over the long haul, satisfy his need (in this case primarily his need for self-esteem), if we know what our goals are, then we can satisfy our various needs by hanging on to those things that are true to our beliefs. The old man's life may have been simpler than ours, it's true, and we may have conflicts he could never have dreamed of out there alone on the high seas. But the similarities are still there. If we understand the need to establish beliefs that are empowering for us and then behave in a manner that's consistent with those beliefs no matter what, we can satisfy our needs and truly get what we want most, just like the old man.

But if we choose to consistently act in a manner that will allow us to satisfy our four needs right now (and remember, satisfying those needs is a daily process), we will always be inclined to take the path of least resistance.

The Path of Least Pain

The path of least resistance is the path that looks inviting and promising. It's the path of least pain, and that's compelling. It's the easiest way to go. For the old man, it meant letting go of the fish so he could rest. For us, it means letting go of hopes and dreams so we can feel good right now.

But it's a path that goes in circles, a path that gets us nowhere. And too often, it's a path that leads us to addictions that ensure we will remain in that circle.

By our definition, an addiction is habitual behavior that produces short-term satisfaction and long-term harm. The reason we have addictions in our lives is because we want to satisfy our four needs now.

Not over time, today.

Addictions are a short-term way of dealing with the threats and symptoms we talked about in the last chapter. They help us deal with the obstacles immediately. Not later, now. Addictions fix things right now. But the problem is, it's only temporary.

Addictions in Their Many Forms

Take a minute and you can think of any number of addictions. Medications are a good example. We've already discussed what a booming business the pain medication business continues to be in this country, and in most cases these medications do nothing to cure what's wrong. Their purpose is to treat the symptoms. When we have a headache and take an aspirin, for instance, we don't really get rid of the root cause of the headache. All the aspirin does is mask the pain so we don't feel it until the reason causing the headache goes away. But the pain is still there. If we never do anything about the obstacle (the problem) that's causing the headache (the symptom) in the first place, the headache will keep returning, and we'll keep going to the medicine cabinet for aspirin. The circle will spin and spin and spin.

Sleeping is a popular, if less visible, addiction. That's one way to keep the obstacles and threats away for a while. Just sleep it off. But are the obstacles and threats gone when we finally decide to wake up?

Avoidance can be another addiction, as well as denial, procrastination, blame, working overtime, and any of thousands of other "masks." Consider each of these potential addictions one by one. All are excellent at masking and delaying pain and keeping our lives stagnant.

Shopping can be an addiction when it's used for the purpose of a short-term satisfaction that masks whatever it is that has the potential of causing us long-term harm. Not only that, it can cost us a lot of money.

How about watching television as an addiction? Americans watch, on the average, nearly thirty-eight hours of TV a week. Why? It's one of the least painful things a person can do—sit and be entertained with your beverage of choice in one hand and a bowl of chips in the other. What's hard about that? Of course, TV isn't the only easy choice that we could be making. According to Nielsen and Pew, Americans spend sixty hours a month surfing the Internet. If you're doing both, that's more than a full-time workweek spent staring at a screen.

What can watching that much television or surfing the Internet get in the way of? Relationships that need work, occupational duties, exercise, making new friends, and the list goes on and on.

Virtually anything can be an addiction if we choose to use it as such. Work can even be an addiction, or family, if we use it in excess as a way of avoiding or delaying things that are important to us.

The Twin Big Ones

Two of the most obvious addictions in our modern society are, of course, alcohol and tobacco. By addictions, I'm not referring to, or entering the debate about, the well-known addictiveness of alcohol and nicotine. In the context of principle-driven behavior, I'm talking about the potential alcohol and tobacco have for allowing us to mask and avoid.

Statistics show that the abuse of these products is enormous. According to the National Institute on Alcohol Abuse and Alcoholism, the cost in dollars alone from alcohol abuse is astronomical:

• Alcohol-related costs to the American society, including medical spending, lost wages, and lost hours of work, total $148 billion a year—the equivalent of fifty-seven cents per drink consumed annually.

Tobacco use isn't far behind in cost of dollars:

• Tobacco rings up a health-care bill of $96 billion and another $97 billion in lost productivity every year according to the Campaign for Tobacco Free Kids.

These aren't statistics that show what Americans are paying merely to purchase and use alcohol and tobacco, they're statistics to show what Americans are paying because of the use of these popular addictions. These costs are just damage control.

Nobody Wins the Addiction Game

The key to understanding addiction is to recognize that it's the culprit that causes us to sacrifice what we want most for what we want now. If we sacrifice what we want most, it will throw us into a vigilant response mode. That vigilant response gets the cortisol flowing because what's happening is unsettling. As time goes on it will typically grind at us more and more; it will compound, build, and agitate. We'll stay in a constant state of anxiety, always preparing for battle (and never going). We'll gear up and get upset and uptight. Then we'll never actually physically battle anything. All that cortisol at work won't do us any good. To the contrary, it will do us a lot of harm if we don't physically exert and rid ourselves of the toxins.

That's just one of the downsides of addictions. They prevent us from dealing with what's hurting us. Most of the time they prevent us from even realizing what it is. The reason why we don't confront the real source of the pain is because we've become slaves to our addictions, whatever ones we might have chosen, and those addictions don't allow us to change our behavior. They mask the pain and call off the fight. They don't allow us to get what we want most. We're always too busy paying attention to and taking care of the now.

Addictions usually start out innocently enough. I like to refer to them in the beginning as Band-Aids. Band-Aids aren't bad in and of themselves. But the problem with Band-Aids is they can become addictions over time. Band-Aids cover up our problems so we don't have to deal with them. If we're not careful, they will completely cover up the signals that tell us there's a problem that needs our attention.

Band-Aids Don't Solve Anything

Think of the warning lights in your car. If you're driving down the street and the "check engine" light comes on, what should you do? Pull over and stop, of course. But do we do that? I know of a person who saw the "check engine" light go on in his car and responded by actually putting a Band-Aid over the light so it wouldn't be annoying. This was a very busy person who couldn't be bothered by that red light, so he reached into the first-aid kit in his glove compartment and took care of the red light. Well, not long after that, his engine burned up. It was drained completely of oil. When the towing company hauled the car to the service department, the mechanics looked inside and there was the Band-Aid, right where it had been left.

We have warning lights go on in our body all the time. In many cases, they are symptoms before they become addictions. If we start to sleep too much, for example, that's probably a warning light that a problem needs to be looked at and dealt with. But too often we'll ignore that warning signal and simply continue to oversleep. As we continue to oversleep, we'll become addicted to that short-term fix. We'll ignore "sleeping" as a warning light and turn it into an addiction—something that helps us mask the pain and feel better now.

In our complex lives we need to be more aware than ever of what's weighing on our minds. It's only when we get in tune with our warning lights that we put ourselves in a position to do something about what turned them on.

Warning Lights Come in Three Convenient Forms

We should also be aware that warning lights generally come on in three different ways. We can see a warning light through a physical response, such as the "check engine" light in the car. Physical response warning lights are the easiest to recognize, understand, and respond to. They are the pains—headaches, stomachaches, tension, chest pains—that tell us something's wrong and we ought to do something about it. Although they are the easiest to recognize, they can also be the most deadly when ignored.

The second way warning lights come on is through emotional responses, such as the desire to oversleep or a chronic habit of denial. Emotional-response warning lights are generally more subtle. They're the ones that require us to be in tune with the beliefs on our Belief Lens and the behavior those beliefs drive. Emotional warning lights come in the form of depression, anxiety, fear, frustration, and anger. They need to be listened to, not ignored.

The third area of warning lights is the one I consider the most important. If you'll recall the Belief Paradigm, you'll remember that we labeled the "mental response" as our trigger. Our mental responses, or self-talks, are the triggers for our behavior. These warning lights are mental responses mostly in the form of self-talks, like the old fisherman had with himself as he went through the ordeal of landing his big fish. Self-talks are the conversations we have with ourselves.

Don't Talk—or Talk Back—Negatively

Very often the reason things cause us distress is because of the negative self-talks we've had about them. We develop negative self-talks because we have a perception of a threat (we're "stressed"), and we conclude we better battle that threat. Thus, a vicious cycle can begin. Surveys have shown that up to 80 percent of our self-talks are negative. If we have negative self-talks going on all the time, then what are we triggering all the time? We're triggering the emotional and physical survival responses as evidenced by the symptoms we've discussed. Then we start to use Band-Aids to cover the symptoms, which, when left unnoticed, can lead to addictions.

Consider building a Community Commerce, or network marketing, business as a source of distress. Why would building a network marketing business stress people out? The most common response is because there is a lot riding on building a successful business. Dreams and goals are centered around creating financial and time independence. Our desire to be with family more while being able to meet their needs—and even some of their wants—can be a major impetus to start building a business; it can also be a major stressor as we worry about building a business that will provide and last. There is also an element of fear and intimidation, that can lead to self-doubt and negativity. What if the business isn't successful? What was I thinking? I can't possibly do this! It will never work out—at least not for me! And because of that, my family will suffer and I'll never achieve my dreams or accomplish my goals.

Now, what happens every time we run the above negative self-talk tapes about our network marketing business failing? We reinforce our belief. Every time we sit down to work on our business, every time we think about sharing the products or opportunity with someone, those are the kind of tapes we run.

We can change our tapes. We have the power to do that. We can create new self-talks that trigger different responses. We can turn the 80 percent negative self-talks into 80 percent positive self-talks, and more. We can recognize the warning lights that come from negative self-talks and eliminate addictions, if we use our self-talks as warning lights and not as negative reinforcement.

Self-Talks Keep Us in Touch with Beliefs

What will our self-talks get us in touch with? They'll get us in touch with our beliefs, of course. When we perceive the building of a network marketing business as a threat because of how much is riding on being successful, we're behaving according to a belief we have that says something along the lines of "My self-worth is tied to whether I'm successful in building this business or not." Since my perception is that I cannot allow myself to fail because there is too much at stake, where does that leave my self-worth? But if in our self-talk we decide to change our belief to "My self-worth is tied to how hard I work, regardless of whether my business immediately takes off," we will satisfy our self-worth need and eliminate the pitfall of addiction.

How about a self-talk regarding this belief: "There is no way I can be successful at this." Since we have already given up, what does that belief inherently imply? We're not going to try very hard to build a successful business, of course. We'll only half-heartedly work on building our business. We'll find ways to procrastinate contacting others. We won't follow up on invitations to home meetings. We won't be very involved with helping downline members grow their businesses, if we even have a downline. All this because we've taken on a belief that says, "There is no way I can be successful."

It's easy to imagine that the results of our behavior will be frustration, cynicism, and probably also exhaustion, since it requires a lot of energy to avoid work. We also won't be very popular with our upline, sideline, and downline.

Since these results hardly qualify as satisfying our needs—in this case our self-esteem and need to live—our self-talks would need to reflect that. We would say to ourselves, "What if I looked at being successful in another way? What if I looked at being successful as trying my hardest, regardless of the outcome? What if being successful wasn't about more money in my pocket, but, instead, it was about helping others to be successful? I would feel better about myself. I would be helping others to make positive changes in their lives. My family would be proud of me and my work." With that kind of self-talk in mind, we're then in a position to change our belief to "Being successful gives me the freedom to move on and be myself."

Self-talk is the trigger that drives new beliefs onto our Belief Lens, enabling us to behave in a manner quite different from our old behavior. Again, this doesn't mean we have to sacrifice our other needs. Our self-talks can also include self-instruction that says advancing in rank isn't the result of our success, but rather the result of the success of those we have helped. This perspective gives us a better sense of self-worth while also providing us the freedom of fulfilling our need for love at home, or our need to enjoy, including at the golf course. That's the beauty of self-talks. They're ours and ours alone. We can talk ourselves into seeing things the way we want to see them for healthy outlooks.

When You Talk, You Usually Listen

There's the story about a guy in the circus whose job was to follow the elephants, camels, and horses on the parade into town and clean up any droppings they happened to leave on the pavement. Somebody watching the parade at the side of the road yells out, "How can you lower yourself like that? How can you perform such a despicable task? Why don't you quit?" To which the circus guy says, "What, and give up show business?"

That's obviously a person who's had some long and effective self-talks.

The world is full of examples of people who use the power of self-talks. We could also call them self-motivators. They are our own internal "halftime speeches." They inspire us to keep a positive attitude, reminding us that we can succeed.

Can you imagine the self-talks Charles Lindbergh must have had as he crossed the Atlantic alone in his airplane? No one else was there to motivate him, to keep him awake and focused. He had to rely on himself. Self-talks are especially important at those moments when we have to decide whether to continue on or abandon ship.

Self-talks can come in many forms. Some people cover their bathroom mirror with slogans, poems, sayings, and other reminders of their goals and beliefs. Others memorize these same slogans, poems, and sayings. In whatever form, their purpose is the same—to keep us in touch with what we want most. They keep us focused. During his professional career, Karl Malone, a basketball player for the Utah Jazz, started chanting to himself just prior to shooting free throws. Although he was accomplished in virtually all other areas of the game, Malone had some difficulty with his free throw percentage, so he turned to self-talks to increase his effectiveness. When asked what he said to himself, he politely declined to reveal the content of those conversations. They were private, he said.

Self-Talks Prevent Overstating Our Troubles

If our self-talks are positive, they'll allow us to look at our lives in ways that are best for us. They'll help us put things in perspective. They'll help us stop short of using big labels for little things. How often in our negative self-talks do we say something is horrible? Well, what's horrible? The famines in Africa. The Holocaust. Right? But is it horrible if someone declines to learn more about a business opportunity? Is it horrible if someone in my downline only recruits one person instead of three? Our self-talks should help us to either use appropriate labels or not label at all. They can have a tremendous impact. I remember walking past a graveyard in Florida and seeing a tombstone with this epitaph: "I Told You I Was Sick." If that's the kind of self-talks the deceased engaged in, maybe he quickened the process.

Our self-talks ought to be positive. They should allow us to see life with hope and enthusiasm, not with dread and foreboding. Hope can spring eternal, when it's internal.

It all ties together when we think about it. To paraphrase Benjamin Franklin: We can't always control what goes on around us, but we can control what goes on inside us.

Instant Replay

Key Points

• The path of least resistance is the path of least pain.

• Addictions satisfy our needs now.

• Our body's warning lights come in three forms: physical, emotional, and mental (self-talks).

• Self-talks are the most important warning light because they trigger our behavior.

Personal Exercise

• Make a list of your warning lights. Have they become an addiction?

Where Do We Go from Here?

In chapter seven, we'll look at the preventive medicine we can all practice to build ourselves mentally, emotionally, and physically.

CHAPTER SEVEN

EXERCISE ONLY ON THE DAYS YOU EAT

Preventive medicine wards off afflictions and effectively deals with the hurdles that get in our way. You can't do more with your life than you are physically, mentally, and emotionally capable of doing.

Now that we've become more aware of the obstacles and threats that are bound to come our way, let's discuss some ways to effectively respond to life's challenges. First, it's important to remember that our responses will come in one of three areas: physical, mental, or emotional, and often a blend of all three. An understanding of the peculiarities of each area is important in outlining an effective principle-based game plan.

Accepting the fact that some obstacles and threats are a necessary fact of life no matter what we do, it follows that it's important to plan in advance those ways to best deal with them. Are there practical, sensible things we can do to make the process easier, to prepare ourselves before the threat comes in and knocks us over? Are there strategies we can put in place that will actually make the journey enjoyable? Are there ways to satisfy our correct principles in spite of the threats? The answer is a resounding Yes!

Remember these six words: A healthy lifestyle is preventive medicine. Or, if you prefer to turn those six words around: Preventive medicine is a healthy lifestyle

Antidote to Addictions

Preventive medicine refers to those things we can do to prepare for whatever obstacles might come our way. It is the antidote to addictions. Preparation enables us to absorb the challenges represented by obstacles; preparation allows us to handle the obstacles instead of them handling us. In many cases, we can actually use the obstacles to make us stronger and to help us grow.

To begin with, I think it's important to appreciate the simple reality that we can only accomplish with our lives what we physically, mentally, and emotionally prepare ourselves to accomplish. We can't go beyond our own preparation and endurance. We can't use magic and mirrors.

It's been said that we can't do more than we are physically capable of doing. Likewise we can't do more than we are emotionally and mentally capable of doing. Hence our mental, emotional, and physical strength is going to determine the limits of our activities and achievements. None of us are superhuman. We have our limits. But it's preparation that helps us stretch our capabilities to their fullest extent. With preparation, we put ourselves in position to be the best we can be.

Let me use this situation to illustrate: If I had two hours of sleep last night, will I respond to the exact same threat differently than if I had eight hours of sleep? Of course I'll respond differently. How much sleep I have will determine how well I can take things on. It will determine how much energy I'll have. If I had two hours of sleep, I'll likely respond irritably and impatiently. If I had eight hours of sleep, I'll likely respond more positively.

Sleep serves as just one simple example of how we can implement a "preventive behavior" that will qualify as preventive medicine. Getting the amount of sleep that's right for us will make us more resilient when it comes to dealing with life's events. By making sure we're well rested, we've reduced our susceptibility to obstacles. We're stronger, more energetic, more patient; we're better able to cope. We're better prepared. When we understand that, then we realize the importance of using sleep as a way to best prepare for the next day, not just as something we do when we're exhausted.

Five General Categories

In general, preventive behaviors tend to fit into one of five categories. These include the areas of fitness and nutrition, finances, relationships, mental and emotional stability, and creativity and expression. Each of these areas greatly impacts our physical, mental, or emotional responses. There are a variety of things we can do not only to avoid the obstacles lurking in each of these areas, but to turn them into positives that will, in turn, bring us inner peace and real harmony as they are fused with the beliefs on our Belief Lens.

Fitness and Nutrition

You, I, and just about everyone in the twenty-first century knows that the hardest part about exercising is getting started. Since we now know about the toxins left in our body because of survival responses, don't we have even more reason to get started? Knowledge can be a wonderful motivator. I would suggest keeping the following list handy, for motivational purposes. Apply these "Ten Tips" in your life, and, if it isn't already, exercise can become a regular—even enjoyable—part of your lifestyle:

1. Give aerobic exercise top priority a minimum of every other day.

2. Identify a variety of aerobic exercises you enjoy. Select two or three different ones to do on a regular basis.

3. Look for a variety of enjoyable places to do your aerobic exercise. Be sure to include alternatives for stormy weather.

4. Choose your best time of day to exercise and be consistent. Remember to wait a minimum of one hour after you eat. Exercising on an empty stomach causes a spike in your blood sugar levels, which leads to your body storing energy in the form of extra fat.

5. Start out slow. Always finish an exercise session feeling like you could have done more, not like you wish you'd never started.

6. Work out to music when possible. Research shows that music actually raises exercise tolerance levels and makes a workout seem easier (which goes a long way in explaining how Rocky always managed to get in shape so fast). Keep the volume on your headphones set to a low level if you're exercising outside, however, so you can hear what's around you (such as big trucks and mad dogs).

7. Work out with a friend or join groups; surround yourself with people who share similar exercise goals.

8. Play at your progress. Do what you did last week a little faster or stronger this week, just a little. Change your courses and challenges regularly for variety.

9. Reward yourself. Every time you work out, for example, pay yourself a dollar, or five dollars. It's your money. Put the money in a special fund for something you really want, like new running shoes.

10. Take an energy inventory. Compare your energy level on the days you work out with the days you don't work out. You may find you're soon working out virtually every day because you realize how much better it makes you feel.

Do It for Health

Of course the best tip of all is to exercise because you want to. For a lot of people—probably a majority of people—that's easier said than realized. For a lot of people, exercise is work, plain and simple; maybe even a necessary evil. But why should we want to exercise? So we can get what we want most, that's why. Exercise is the most effective way to avoid the contraction band lesions we talked about in chapter four. It's the most effective way to lower blood pressure. It's the most effective way to have healthy hearts. The benefits are legend. How can we get what we want most if we don't have our physical health? Remember the results of the University of North Carolina study in chapter two, where the four thousand retired executives lamented "throwing away my health as if it were trash." With the proper use of self-talks, it's possible to actually want to exercise.

Let's talk about blood pressure and heart disease, two of the most prevalent health threats of the twenty-first century. The best way to lower blood pressure and reduce the risk of heart disease is to strengthen the heart muscle. Build it up. Make it so strong that when your doctor listens to it he gets a huge smile on his face. The stronger your heart, the more blood it can pump with each stroke. The more blood the heart is capable of pumping with each stroke, the lower your blood pressure and the lower your resting heart rate. For strong hearts, the tugs and pulls of everyday life become a piece of cake, so to speak. It's easy to get a good read on just how strong your heart is by measuring your resting pulse rate. When you're stationary and relaxed, look at your watch or a clock and put your index finger on a major blood vessel, such as the jugular vein in your neck. Count the number of beats for ten seconds. Then multiply by six to get the number of times your heart beats per minute. Between seventy and eighty beats per minute is considered normal. Anything over that indicates a heart that needs strengthening. Anything under seventy indicates a stronger than average heart. Below sixty is getting stronger.

Below fifty is better yet. Below forty and you might consider entering the next Boston Marathon or Tour de France.

Bear in mind that aerobic exercise is anything we do that raises our heartbeat to our target heart rate for at least twenty minutes. Whenever we engage in aerobic exercise we work out our heart muscle.

When it comes to training your heart, there are two types of exercise that you should use: fat-burning and high intensity or interval training. Fat burning exercise is any exercise that is steady and consistent. Walking, hiking, climbing stairs, or swimming are all examples of fat-burning exercise. They key is to reach that elevated heart rate without getting out of breath. Shoot for somewhere between 130–140 beats per minute. High intensity training—like sprinting (either on the track, on a bike, or in the pool)—utilizes bursts of explosive activity followed by periods of recovery. Each interval of high intensity should last for approximately one minute with the goal of reaching 150–170 beats per minute followed by rest periods of around one to two minutes that allow your heart rate to drop to 120–130 beats. Fat-burning exercise, as the name suggests, burns fat while high-intensity training burns sugar. So try to do your high-intensity training before you do fat burning—this will allow you to burn more fat during your fat-burning exercise.

When I was in college, I got a very vivid education as to the results of aerobic exercise when they gave echocardiograms to the track team. We had a big guy from Sweden on our team who threw the shot put and he and I went for our echocardiograms at the same time. When our tests were done they took the pictures they'd taken of our hearts and backlit them so we could see what they looked like. The shot putter was about twice as big as me, with these huge muscles all over his body that were twice as big as mine. But my heart muscle was twice as big as his. Why? I like to think it's because I'm all heart. What those echocardiograms really showed was that I regularly worked out aerobically, and he did not.

The shot putter worked out with huge weights that built up his biceps, his triceps, his quads, and his deltoids. I worked out by running long distances, and that mostly built up my heart. The muscles we worked all the time were big and strong; the ones we paid little attention to weren't so big and strong. It's that simple. In the long run, the heart muscle is the most important. It won't get you many stares on the beach, but it will keep you going to the beach for a long, long time.

Mix It Up

Of course, modern physiologists have found that a mixture of aerobic exercise with weight lifting can be a most effective combination. Working with weights develops lean muscle mass, and the body will respond with a higher metabolic rate anytime it has additional muscle mass to support. Aerobic exercise mixed with weight work gives the body a kind of double signal to increase its metabolism.

The beauty of aerobic exercise is that it doesn't have to be overly time-consuming for maximum results. Thirty minutes a day at your target heart rate will maintain a high level of fitness. If you want to train for a marathon or a century bike race, or if you want to swim the English Channel or climb Mount Everest, fine. That may be the best kind of motivation to keep your interest level high. But it isn't necessary. All the body asks is consistent maintenance. You don't even need to exercise every day. Exercise only on the days you eat. Give it thirty minutes every day, and the rewards can be tremendous. Give it more than that, and the results will build even more.

Aerobic exercise also goes well beyond working out the heart muscle. Done regularly, it also does the following:

- Reduces levels of so-called bad cholesterol (Low-Density Lipoproteins) and increases levels of good cholesterol (High-Density Lipoproteins).

- Changes your food cravings from fats and sugars to the fuel foods, or carbohydrates.

- Raises your metabolic rate.

The last two are especially significant because they apply positively to nutrition and weight loss—two very common concerns in our modern lives. Indeed, the preoccupation with being overweight is not just one of the biggest concerns in our modern society but also one of our biggest stressors. It demands a great deal of time, attention, and concern that could otherwise be placed elsewhere.

Starvation Isn't Worth It

The whole key to how much fat your body carries is your metabolic rate, or the base rate at which your body burns calories. It follows, then, that the key to weight loss is raising your metabolic rate. The higher the rate, the more fat you burn. Now think about this for a minute. If you go on a starvation diet, what do you do to your metabolic rate? You slow it down. What kind of foods does your body crave? Right, sugars and fats. The reason it craves the high-calorie sugars and fats is because they can be stored and later used as fuel. When you're starving yourself, your body instinctively goes into a survival mode to protect you from starvation. It doesn't know the difference between a diet and a famine. When no food is coming in, it intuitively lowers its metabolic rate and sends out alarm signals for sugars and fats. That's why restrictive calorie diets don't work. Sooner or later the body will take over and go on a sugar and fat binge, piling all the weight back on. Studies have shown that 90 percent of people who go on a starvation diet actually weigh more a year later.

If this information stops you from ever going on a restrictive calorie diet, that's great. Take the information a step further. If metabolic rate determines how much fat your body burns, then what will be the only truly effective diet? Anything that raises your metabolic rate is the answer. What raises your metabolic rate? Exercise, that's what. Just as your body will overcompensate in the face of a starvation diet—shutting down beyond where it needs to—it will overcompensate in the other direction when you exercise.

Not only will you burn more calories because you're exercising, but by raising your base metabolic rate you'll burn more calories all the time. You'll burn them at a higher rate when you're resting, even when you're sleeping. After aerobic exercise, your body doesn't immediately lower its metabolic rate. You experience what's known as a post-workout burn, and your metabolic rate will only come down gradually over a forty-eight-hour period. If you exercise again within that forty-eight-hour period, you never go back to the metabolic rate you were at before you started exercising. Pretty soon you've raised your bottom level. If you keep exercising, it keeps going up, at least to a point. This is why people at their ideal weight eat more than people who are overweight and still don't gain weight.

If you try to lose weight permanently without exercising you might as well beat your head against the wall, because your body doesn't know how to do it. You're essentially fighting a losing battle against nature.

Another critical key to weight loss is balancing your blood sugar levels. Your body burns glucose to fuel every movement you make. That fuel is transported via your blood. When you maintain consistent levels of blood sugar, your body will run the way it was meant to. When your blood sugar levels are out of whack, your body will respond by storing sugar as body fat.

Here's what happens. When you starve your body—as I mentioned above—your blood sugar levels drop and your body stores more energy as fat in order to protect itself against future shortages. So, when you skip a meal, restrict calories or carbohydrates, or exercise on an empty stomach, your blood sugar levels drop and your body protects its stores of fat energy. This in turn causes your body to burn muscle for fuel (which lowers your metabolic rate) and causes more intense cravings for fatty and high calorie foods.

On the flip side, when you overeat, your blood sugar levels spike. With no outlet for all that extra fuel, your body stores it as fat to use later.

But when your blood sugar levels are balanced, your body is in a happy state of homeostasis. When balanced, your body will release fat as fuel and protect lean muscle. You'll also notice fewer cravings even as you feel increased levels of energy.

That's why, more and more, you're hearing the advice to eat several smaller meals rather than the traditional three big meals a day. Spreading your meals out throughout the day in five to six small meals helps to maintain a constant and consistent blood sugar level. Your body craves that constancy and consistency, and when it has it, your body feels more secure. When your body is secure, it doesn't have to protect itself as much, allowing it to function properly.

Now that we've talked about preparing ourselves physically through exercise and nutrition, let's move to another response area that's more emotionally oriented.

Finances

You might wonder what finance has to do with emotion, but isn't it chiefly our emotions that come into play when we're dealing with finances? If we have our finances under control, then our emotions will be in better control as well, and vice versa. The world doesn't seem like such a threatening place when we're fiscally fit.

In a book called *Uncommon Cents*, author Lynn Robbins offers some interesting perspectives on how we often look at finances and how we ought to look at finances. He makes a list of "The Seven Deadly Myths About Money," and I think they make a lot of sense and should be included here.

Consider the seven myths and their corresponding principles:

MYTH 1: MORE MONEY WILL SOLVE MY MONEY PROBLEMS.
Principle: Greater income than outgo will solve my money problems.

MYTH 2: FOLLOWING A BUDGET INHIBITS MY FREEDOM OF CHOICE.

Principle: Following a budget brings greater control over important choices.

MYTH 3: THE CHECKBOOK BALANCE IS MY BEST SPENDING BAROMETER.
Principle: The checkbook balance cannot forecast the unexpected.

MYTH 4: I SPEND ACCORDING TO MY NEEDS.
Principle: Most people spend according to emotion.

MYTH 5: GOING INTO DEBT GIVES ME CHOICES NOW INSTEAD OF HAVING TO WAIT.
Principle: Going into debt decreases my future options.

MYTH 6: MONEY IS INTRINSICALLY VALUABLE.
Principle: Money can only be exchanged for things of value.

MYTH 7: MY PRESENT FINANCIAL SITUATION IS A RESULT OF CIRCUMSTANCES AND EVENTS OUT OF MY CONTROL.
Principle: My present financial situation is a result of decisions I made based on the money principles I believe in.

Robbins notes that this list isn't all-inclusive when it comes to money myths, but he gets his point across. Financial control is all about fitting principles onto our Belief Lens and then acting accordingly. It's when we fail to recognize our financial principles, or even know what they are, that we can get into financial difficulties. Applying time-proven principles ahead of time is preventive medicine that will eliminate the unnecessary stressors of financial concerns.

More Money Tips

One of the things I love about the Community Commerce business model is that your success is primarily dependent on the success of others. In other words, I succeed when you succeed. The great leaders that I have worked with have truly understood this principle. I can't tell you how many times I've seen people who didn't have the résumés or background to suggest that they would be successful. But, through helping others to be successful, they've been able to achieve fantastic results. What's more, I've never seen any group of people have more fun doing what they're doing than the people I've worked with through MonaVie.

My experiences have led me to come up with a short list of empowering beliefs regarding how to realize financial control in our lives. Consider the following:

- Personal commitment and motivation are more important than degrees and background.

- My success is a natural result of helping others to be successful.

- If you aren't enjoying what you're doing, then you most likely will not succeed and you're wasting your time.

When we're free of financial constraints, and we're exercising properly and regularly, we're in better shape to turn our attention to those significant people around us with whom we seek to have enduring, satisfying and, in some cases, lasting relationships.

Relationships

This is another area that has a tremendous impact on us emotionally. In understanding relationships, it's helpful to understand the concept of value. Most of us have a misconception about value. We've bought into the idea that value is intrinsic, that worth is innate and will always be there. In the common view, value is seen as some kind of inherent quality that exists in a person, item, process, or service. After all, isn't gold intrinsically valuable? But in reality, value is not something intrinsic or innate at all. Value is achieved only through a complementary exchange of satisfaction of needs.

In applying this understanding to relationships, we can realize the importance of a value exchange. Only when there is a healthy exchange of values in both directions can there be a healthy relationship.

We cannot underestimate the need for relationships. Think about it. All of our needs are primarily met through relationships. Whether the need is for food, love, or to feel important, other people are most often relied upon to help us meet these needs. It's when these needs are met that relationships have value.

You establish a marriage relationship because you receive more value by being married than by being single. It enhances your life. It makes it better. There's real value there. Likewise, you have the same garage service your car every time because you value that the repairs are done right at a fair cost, or even because you value the convenience of the garage's location. Whatever the reason, you have a relationship with the people who operate that garage, and you will continue the relationship as long as it is of value to you.

One of the key aspects of Community Commerce is implied in its name: community. While it is true that Community Commerce represents an incredible opportunity to build a successful business, many people join—and many more thrive—because of the associations and relationships that come from being involved with people with similar goals and dreams. Community Commerce represents a very viable means of satisfying a need for positive relationships.

It's when we fail to receive enough value that we question the need for relationships. Marriages end in divorce when there is no longer enough value being received, by one party or the other, or both. If you change garages it's because the quality declines or the prices become too high, or some other negative arises that decreases the value of that relationship. Many distributors quit Community Commerce because an upline, sideline, or downline quits, or because something happens to taint a relationship created through Community Commerce.

By being aware of value, we can service our relationships better and be more conscious of the values we ourselves contribute. We will be motivated to work on skills of communication, intimacy, and selflessness. We will strive always to increase, not decrease, our value in our "valued" relationships, which will improve our mental and emotional stability.

Mental and Emotional Stability

Being generally mentally and emotionally stable gives us the basis for a solid life that isn't at the whim of outside forces we would otherwise have no control over. Only with a solid mental and emotional foundation can we deal with the obstacles of modern life and actually find the time to thrive.

Mental and emotional stability gives us something I view as very important—the time for valuable self-talks that we can use to enhance our self-worth. Refer to this list of "A Dozen Affirmations" to keep you on the right track in regard to positive self-talking:

1. I am a valuable, kind person; I am worthy of the respect of others.

2. I am my own best friend; I nurture myself with exercise, healthful nutrition, and effective time management.

3. I enjoy my own company; I have a good sense of humor and can forgive myself when I make errors.

4. I love myself unconditionally; by loving myself I will have love to give to others.

5. I accept compliments easily and readily give them to others.

6. I allow myself to feel my feelings and express them in healthy ways.

7. I set my goals clearly. I accept any setbacks as opportunities to learn and as part of the process of my growth.

8. I hear, see, and believe in all that is positive, healthy, and helpful to myself and others.

9. I know negative thoughts and feelings deprive me of productive energy; I choose to be positive and productive.

10. I am compassionate, kind, truthful, and patient with myself and others.

11. I focus on that which I can directly control; I let go of worry and the things I cannot control or change.

12. I have plenty of time; I am organized, productive, and aware of my priorities.

Life Is Full of Negatives

If we subscribe to this list on a daily basis, the goal of mental and emotional stability can't help but be squarely in our sights. We can counteract the bombardment of negatives thrown at us daily. *The Wall Street Journal* once published a report that said that every day by two in the afternoon, school-aged kids had already received an average of 118 negative impressions about themselves. Like it or not, that's the kind of society in which we live. It's full of negatives. We hear them all the time—about ourselves, about others. Where are we if we don't have a personal course of preventive medicine that counters with at least an equal number of positive impressions?

I would like to add a personal endorsement to number three on the list above, specifically the part about humor. I believe a healthy sense of humor can be one of the best preventive medicines we can prescribe for ourselves. It's instructive that doctors have discovered a direct correlation between the immune system and a sense of humor. Norman Cousins is famous for his book *Anatomy of an Illness*, in which he describes having a degenerative disease and getting healthy again by taking vitamin C and watching funny videos.

We need to pay close attention to how much and how often we laugh. Studies show that the average child laughs four hundred times a day. The average adult laughs sixteen times a day. That's a serious decline, and for our own good it ought to be reversed. Laughter enhances our self-esteem; it boosts our sense of wellbeing. We should look for opportunities to laugh genuinely. We should make that a priority. We should associate with people who laugh and who help us see the humorous side of life. We should study children more and see what it is they have that we might have lost along the way.

The more pleasantly we view life, the more we'll have a yearning for creativity and expression.

Creativity and Expression

This is the last of the areas we want to cover in our look at preventive behaviors. It's the area that prompts us to focus inward and ask the following questions of ourselves:

- What do I really want?

- What activities have value for me?

- What do I really enjoy doing and sharing?

- What was I doing and how was I acting the last time I felt a complete sense of harmony and inner peace?

These questions are neither quickly nor easily answered. But pondered objectively they can help us understand what we want out of life and what excites us. As a result, we'll have a desire to become ourselves, rather than what others—or our environment—want us to be.

This "conformity to self" can be a real prison break. We'll stop conforming to other people's values and conform to our own values. We'll satisfy ourselves and not spend all our time trying to satisfy expectations that others may have for us.

We've all noticed that some people seem to have a certain magic in their approach to life. They have the uncanny ability to be at the right place at the right time and are always falling into opportunities and successes seemingly by accident, while the rest of us watch in disbelief and frustration. That frustration is only heightened when these people don't seem to be at all aware of what they're doing. They casually stroll up and grab the brass ring we've been knocking ourselves out trying to get.

Conform to Yourself

The secret to understanding those who seem to have the magic lies in applying the principles of conformity. Very likely they have bought into their own beliefs, their own values, and not someone else's. They realize they are unique. Not feeling a need to conform to anyone other than ourselves—within reason of course—can open up doors of creativity and expressiveness previously locked. We're at our best when we're ourselves, when we're aware of our own uniqueness.

Once we're aware of our own uniqueness, we're in a much better position to balance all of the conflicting goals, needs, desires, and duties inherent in our lives. Balance is a key preventive behavior. With true balance in our lives we feel even further in control, and we're able to fill our many roles with a higher level of personal satisfaction. It is possible to be good spouses, good parents, good sons and daughters, good employees, good supervisors, good club members, good church members, and good taxpayers all at the same time, but only if we understand the need to balance. An overemphasis on any of the priorities in our lives can lead to an "out-of-round" life that satisfies some needs at the expense of others. We can't be two places at once. We can't invent more time. We can't be all things to all people.

Knowing what our human capabilities are and attending to them accordingly makes us masters and not slaves. Behavior can either lead, or it can follow. In the case of the addictions we talked about previously, it's a matter of behavior following the addictions. In the case of the measures of preparation talked about in this chapter, it's a matter of behavior leading the way to satisfactory results.

Instant Replay

Key Points

- A healthy lifestyle is preventive medicine.

- Preventive measures fit into these five categories: fitness and nutrition, finances, relationships, mental and emotional stability, and creativity and expression.

- Only exercise on days you eat.

- Believe it or not, we can control money.

- Relationships work when there is an exchange of values.

- Positive self-talks can do wonders to drown out the negativity of the world.

- Don't conform to others, conform to yourself!

Personal Exercise

- Identify a financial myth currently operating in your life. Make a list of specific behaviors you can do to live by a time-proven principle.

- Keep an Exercise Log.

- Keep a Personal Food Record.

Where Do We Go from Here?

In chapter eight, we'll look at choices in a new light—not as something we have to do, but as something we get to do.

CHAPTER EIGHT

THE CHOICES ARE ALL OURS

If you can find a better path, take it! Each of us makes the decisions about where we want to go and how we want to get there. It's up to us and no one else.

By implementing preventive behaviors as outlined in the previous chapter, there's a marvelous side benefit that comes as a result of our resultant new control: we are able to really get in touch with what we want most.

It's a process of self-awareness, and it goes in orderly steps. Recognizing warning lights is the first step. By getting in touch with the appropriate signals, we're moving in the right direction. Then comes preventive behavior. That's followed by a keener awareness of who we are, where we are, and, most important, where we want to go.

Once we know where it is we want to go, we put ourselves in a position to choose the right paths. When there is no destination, or when the destination is hazy at best, our choices of pathways don't amount to much more than the flip of a coin. As the saying goes, "No wind favors he who has no destined port." How many people spend their days walking around in circles, winding up at the end of the day at the exact same spot they found themselves the day before? Or even in a worse spot? How many addictions keep us from going anywhere except where we've already been?

Lindbergh's Landing

The solo trans-Atlantic airplane flight of Charles Lindbergh stands as one of the most famous events in aviation history, and not because of Lindbergh's takeoff on May 20, 1927, at 7:52 A.M., from an airplane hangar at Roosevelt Field in New York. The reason Lindbergh and his plane, the Spirit of St. Louis, are legendary is because of the landing he made at Paris's Le Bourget airport thirty-three hours and thirty-two minutes later. It's the destination that put everything in focus. Lindbergh knew that just taking off wasn't good enough, and, in fact, without meticulous planning, it could have been disastrous. He knew he had just enough fuel, and he hoped enough endurance, to make it to that exact touchdown spot in France. His flight plan was direct and to the point. No detours. No side trips. From the moment he left New York he knew where he was going, and everything he did along the way was designed to keep the journey going in a straight line. He became famous because he knew where he was going. And, that's precisely where he wound up.

Of course that's an easy example with both a tangible start and a tangible finish. Most of the destinations in our own lives—the things we want most—aren't tangible like that. Rather, they are ideals and goals that guide and shape our lives. They are those motivators that keep us excited and enthused about living. Intangible as they might be, we can nonetheless fix on our goals as tightly as Lindbergh fixed on Paris.

To me, the great golfer Jack Nicklaus serves as an excellent example of goal focusing in the sports-minded twentieth century. I was watching an interview once when a reporter asked Nicklaus, who at that point had won nineteen major golf championships in his career, if he knew where he stood in relationship to the all-time greats of golf. Nicklaus had just finished his round that day and was, I presumed, off to dinner or to relax, and perhaps that's why I remember his answer so well. He didn't just give a short reply and hurry on, as is usually the case in such situations. He pondered the question and then affirmed that, yes, as a matter of fact, he knew exactly where he stood in relationship to the all-time greats of golf. He knew that Bobby Jones had won thirteen major championships, Ben Hogan had won eleven, Byron Nelson had won ten, and Arnold Palmer had won eight. He knew that his nineteen amounted to more than anyone in history, but he also knew that didn't mean somebody wouldn't come along some day and surpass what he had done. In fact, he said he fully expected that would happen, and he wouldn't be surprised if it happened in his lifetime. It was his belief that now that he had come along and taken Bobby Jones's mark and extended it into a further orbit, it would give the next generation a higher target to shoot at.

I thought Jack Nicklaus revealed two significant things that day about himself and about goal setting:

One, his career had not been built on chance and happenstance. From the day he won his first major championship at the age of twenty-two, up to that very moment, he knew what he wanted most. And he'd devoted all the energy he could to getting it.

Two, he knew the value of having a target in sight. He knew the importance of having something to shoot at, a verification that what you're aiming at is indeed reachable.

This interview was when Nicklaus was in his mid-forties, his prime playing days supposedly well behind him. I remember thinking as he concluded that interview that he just might win another major championship if he could, just to push that orbit out a little further and make it more of a challenge for those following in his wake. It was obvious that winning majors was his passion. That goal was still in front of him. That's what drove him. That's what kept him energized. A year later, when at the age of forty-six Jack Nicklaus became the oldest man to ever win the Masters and, in the process, run his list of major championship wins to twenty, I was not surprised. This was a man who knew where he was going and what he wanted most, and as a consequence got it.

As a postscript, I might add that I was also not surprised when Jack Nicklaus turned fifty not long after winning that Masters and showed little enthusiasm for the Senior Golf Tour. He really had no incentive for the senior tour because it offered him no path to the goals he had so firmly entrenched in his mind. They don't play major championships on the senior tour.

Direction from Within

Our pursuits may not be so famous or public as Charles Lindbergh's or Jack Nicklaus', and certainly not as one-dimensional, but that doesn't mean they aren't as meaningful and as lofty. The idea behind destinations and goal setting is they give our lives direction from within. They're meaningful and lofty because of their importance to us. If we view them as important, then they are important. It's as simple as that.

Direction should not be confused with rigidity. Our lives needn't be conservative straight lines, never deviating, always on a fixed course. In fact, well-roundedness demands exactly the opposite. Getting caught up in the "one goal" syndrome is a hazard we should be aware of and take great care to avoid. In truth, our lives are multifaceted, and as we seek to fill our basic needs, we are required to fill many roles. The important thing is to focus and concentrate on those facets and those roles that constitute for us a healthy, balanced life.

What Is Valuable to You?

Take a minute to jot down a list of those things that you personally believe are essential to a healthy and balanced life. In general terms, such lists typically include things like meaningful relationships, professional satisfaction, an acceptable level of education, excellent health, things to look forward to (vacations, etc.), and quality time for favorite recreational pursuits and hobbies.

Now think of these items in terms of the Belief Paradigm. Are they needs, beliefs, behaviors, or results? When I have asked this question of people, more often than not I'll get responses that these things are results and sometimes even behaviors. I know this is something of a trick question, since any of these answers could be correct depending on your definition. The correct answer in this instance is that they are beliefs. How can I be so sure they're beliefs? Because that was what was asked for in the first place. Remember, I asked for a list of those things you personally believe are essential to a healthy and balanced life.

In other words, your list is what you believe you want most in your life—the things we value most. These beliefs or values are simply people's views about how they can best meet their needs over time. It's just a perception, but it's a powerful perception because it's based on your life's experiences.

Could you have values that hinder you? Yes! Over time you may find that what you identified as a value today wound up driving behavior that didn't meet your needs over time.

When you identify your values, I believe it's important to make sure you have values that relate to and meet all four of your needs. If you do not have values established for one or more of your needs, you will lead an unhealthy and unbalanced life. How many people do you know who are one-dimensional and lament what's lacking in their lives? They may spend all their energy on a relationship, on their job, or on a hobby because they never focused and established a value in other areas of their lives. It's important that all our needs are addressed.

Remember, life's experiences are all we have to go by when establishing our values and beliefs. We get them from our parents, from the society we live in, from our surroundings, from our churches. In sum, we get our values and beliefs from whatever we're exposed to all of our lives.

Our Values Are Our Destinations

It's these values and beliefs that become our destinations. They become what we want most. By being in touch with them (the closer the better) not only are we able to choose the right paths, but the obstacles in our lives, instead of being nothing but useless distractions, actually make a transformation and become what we view as necessary distractions.

If we're secure that the paths we're following fit into our beliefs, then following those paths will be valuable to us—threats, obstacles, and all. If the paths we're following don't fit into our beliefs, it only follows that we'd want to quit following them.

A good example is our jobs. We choose to work where we're working because we believe it will maximize our circumstances to achieve what we want most in life. That needs to be a given for us. It's our choice. If we don't believe where we're working is maximizing our potential, why work there? Lee Iacocca, former president and CEO of Chrysler, famously said that if you can find a better car, buy it. I say if you can find a better path in your life, take it. Get off the path you're on now and get on a better one if you have a better one available to you. The point is, it's our decision, and what we choose is because of a belief that that choice will maximize what we want most in life.

A Major Change

This point hit home very poignantly for one man who had spent his life developing a reputation as the hardest worker at his company. He was an ironworker, and he worked at two speeds: fast and faster. His job was his life. If there was a chance for overtime—and there usually was—he was the first to volunteer. He routinely worked Saturdays and Sundays. When he would finally go home, he would work on his house or his cars. He only stopped to eat and sleep, and sometimes just barely. Every year his allotted vacation time went unused.

As you might assume, this devotion to work brought with it some casualties. His first marriage had dissolved, and his second marriage was on shaky ground. He'd developed very poor relationships with his children, and the same thing was happening all over with his grandchildren.

Then this hardworking ironworker was introduced to the concept of principle-driven behavior. For the first time in his life, after more than thirty-five years of hard work, he looked at the choices he was making and, more significantly, at the beliefs driving those choices. During the course of his examination he came to the conclusion that he had a belief on his Belief Lens that said you had to work constantly in order to provide for your family. Further examination revealed that this belief was a result of an upbringing during the Great Depression, when his father and mother worked almost around the clock to keep their family clothed and fed.

That hard-work belief had been strongly imprinted on this man's mind, and it drove his choices to work hard even if it meant sacrificing virtually every other area of his life. By being true to this belief, he'd succeeded in satisfying his need to live. No one could argue that. But it was at the exclusion of too many other needs.

He changed his belief to one that said hard work was important only to a point and that families needed to be provided for in more ways than financially. He cut back to forty hours a week. He turned down overtime. He took every minute of vacation time he had coming. He went places with his family and left work behind. Those were his new choices, and they were choices driven by his new belief. It wasn't easy at first. Hard work can be a very compelling habit. As he cut back, he found that the results were as dramatic as they were positive. His marriage improved. He developed relationships with his grandchildren he had never enjoyed with his own children when they were young, and he mended fences with his children as well. All because he'd gone through the Belief Paradigm and found his values and beliefs were out of whack. The plan he put together, based on his new beliefs, adjusted all that, and he found a peace and contentment he'd never known before.

This same story plays out time and again in the Community Commerce industry. I could create tome upon tome of stories of individuals who left unhappy professional situations to join MonaVie. The details may be different—lack of time with family, poor pay, no opportunity to progress, etc., etc.—but the stories remain the same. By changing their beliefs regarding their current situation and their beliefs regarding Community Commerce, these people enabled themselves to venture out into a new opportunity.

We all have different circumstances. We need to look at them, whatever they might be, and take care to make sure our choices maximize what we want most in our lives. We should select our jobs based on that. We should select where we live, and how, based on what's best for our needs. Then we have ownership for where we're working and what we're doing. If you've got something better to do, do it. If you want to live off the land, then get out of the city; go do it. Don't complain about all the stuff you have to put up with every day as a result. It's your life; it's your choice. You chose it because it brings you certain benefits.

For example, I have many times asked in large groups, who has the longest commute to work. After identifying the winner, I ask, "Why do you commute so far?" The reasons are because they can live in a more desirable neighborhood, in a rural setting, or because it's closer to family. The point is, even though traffic is a stressor, it's OK with them because of the benefits that accompany it.

The key is to focus on the benefits and on making good choices, not on the obstacles.

I think it's important to note that ownership doesn't necessarily mean having some kind of physical title. It's a mental freeing up, a crystal clear perception that we're in charge of what we're doing.

Everyone Feels Like an Owner

One of the biggest success stories in American business annals is the Marriott Corporation. What began as an A&W Root Beer stand in Washington, D.C., in 1927, has grown into one of the world's largest and most profitable food service and lodging corporations. Marriott hotels circle the globe, and the Marriott food services arm is ever present, catering to airlines, businesses, and corporations.

After being named Chief Executive of the Year by a national magazine, the CEO of the Marriott Corp, J. Willard Marriott, Jr., son of the empire's founder, credited any success Marriott has had to a firmly held company principle that every employee would be treated as if he or she owned the company.

"My father started the tradition," said J. Willard Marriott, Jr., "by knowing the names and family histories of every employee." While the junior Marriott admitted that with over 200,000 employees, knowing everyone's name and history wasn't literally possible anymore, the principle still held.

"We're still a family," he said. "Our mandate is the same now as it was in the beginning: Treat the employees in ways that cause them to create extra customer service. We want to take care of our employees so that they will want to take care of our customers."

The Marriott CEO shared a few of the principles his father handed down. They included:

- My greatest resource is my staff. If I stop listening, they stop talking, and then I lose their input.

- You can't manage a business by sitting in an office.

- Letting your employee know you care has to be part of your daily life, not just something you do once in a while.

- Don't forget the basics. Don't cook the pancakes in advance and put them on the steam table.

- The greatest reward you can give an employee is a pat on the back and telling them they're doing a good job. "We've found that money is well down the list of criteria for job satisfaction," said Marriott.

The above is no doubt why the Marriott Corporation, still a family-owned business, has done what most family businesses do not do—survived the second generation.

Marriott employees may be just that—employees—but they're treated as if they own the place.

Ownership Has Its Privileges

It's important to feel that sense of ownership. The beauty is, once we've established ownership, once we've put ourselves in charge, we can deal with what we have to deal with. If we don't assume that ownership, we're doomed before we start. We're going to be constantly stressed out, frustrated, and disappointed. Struggles will be the norm. It will always be what everybody else is doing to us. Others will be to blame. We can't buy a break. Life won't be fair, and on and on.

When we assume ownership, we look at the same things that might have stressed us out and frustrated and disappointed us in the past and see them as part of the process to obtain what we want most in our lives. When that's the case, we can put up with the threats and the obstacles. We can work with them because we know they're along the path to our destination, and that's our choice. That's what we've decided to do.

Instant Replay

Key Points

- To choose the right path, we need to first know where it is we want to end up.

- All of our circumstances are different; choose paths that will maximize whatever your circumstances happen to be.

- When we're in touch with our needs, our choices will always be directed toward satisfying those needs.

- If you can find a better path, take it!

Personal Exercise

• Make a list of the elements of a healthy, balanced life (what you want most in life). Are you on a path (personally and professionally) to achieve what you want?

Where Do We Go from Here?

In chapter nine, we'll consider what we can control and, just as important, what we can't.

CHAPTER NINE

CONTROL WHAT YOU CAN
AND WHAT YOU CAN'T

Once we have chosen our life's path, we are then in a better position to control our responses to obstacles we find on those paths by implementing empowering beliefs.

How we handle the necessary obstacles and threats in our lives—the ones we've decided we'll accept and deal with as part of the process to meet our needs—is determined by the degree of control we have over those events. We need to always keep in mind that if any given event or obstacle is not part of the path that maximizes our circumstances, we need to eliminate it from our lives. It's the remaining events we need to learn to deal with.

Again, understanding is the key. In this case, understanding where the events in our lives fit into the spectrum of things we can control and those we can't. Every event in our lives can be assigned to one of three categories. The first category is those events that we have little or no control over; the second category is those obstacles we have partial control over; and the third category is those obstacles we have total or almost total control over. Obviously, the borders that separate these three categories are soft ones. With some obstacles, it's hard to decide exactly where they belong, while with others we find they're about halfway between categories and we could accurately say that they belong to both.

If we were to take our master list of events or obstacles and place them individually in the category where we think they belong, we can get a grasp on which ones should be getting our attention when it comes to control and which ones shouldn't.

It sounds elementary, and it is, but it's imperative that we know how much control we have over a given obstacle before we try to control that obstacle. If we have absolutely no control, then it follows that it's fruitless, not to mention depressing and a waste of time, to try to exercise any control. Conversely, if we have total control, then it's expedient that we exercise that control. To not do so wouldn't be in our best interest.

Let's take an example using, once again, Community Commerce. In which category do we put building a network marketing business? Well, it depends on the opportunity, of course. Very rigid, restrictive programs and systems would fit into the "no control" category, while opportunities that allow more latitude to implement ideas might fit squarely in the "partial control" category. Some opportunities might even fit into the "total control" category, but probably only if you have complete freedom to do whatever you see fit with little or no supervision.

For the sake of this example, let's say that we are part of a program that is very rigid and controlling and one we don't think allows for our own creativity very much. So we've decided to put this opportunity in the "no control" category. With that done, we might say, "So what?" If the situation created by the opportunity isn't controllable by us, then what does it matter where we put it?

It matters because when we know how much control we have, we can then act—or not act—accordingly.

If we have absolutely no control over the programs and systems, why would we ever want to beat our heads against the wall trying to have some control over them? It's good that we realize we have no control. We need to know that so we won't try to exert any.

Keep in mind that our job is a given. We've chosen to do what we do because we have decided it is the best path available to us to maximize what we want most in our life. We believe that. That's our decision. We're willing to deal with any necessary obstacles that might be associated with our job. Since we've decided that how the opportunity is conducted is one of those necessary obstacles, and we've further decided that the programs and systems are totally out of our control, the only way we can coexist peacefully with the opportunity is to accept our limitations. We can't control the situation, so let's not try. Let's not waste our time and make our lives anxious and frustrated as a result.

Partial Control

Let's take another example. This time we'll use our old friend, "traffic." Let's say we decide that traffic, whether we like it or not, is an obstacle we can only partially control. We've decided there are some things we can do about traffic, at least to a point. For starters, we could commute to work before or after rush hour. We could find another route home that's less crowded. We could buy foreign language CDs and listen to them while stuck in traffic, thereby turning a negative into a positive. Those are all things we could decide to do that are under our control.

But we can't drive other people's cars, and we can't make other people carpool and leave their cars home. We don't have control over people cutting in front of us on the freeway, not using their turn signals, or driving slow in the fast lane. We can drive ourselves crazy (no pun intended) thinking we can make decisions for other people about their driving habits, but in reality that's their control, not ours.

So we've thought about it, and we've got a pretty good idea where our control starts and where it stops in regard to traffic. Now what? We accept both sides, that's what. We control what we can control, and we leave alone what we can't. The obstacle is identified, quantified, and actualized. That done, the threat of traffic won't surprise us every day. The traffic won't set our teeth on edge and it won't ruin our day because we know what to expect. We're prepared to control what we can and not worry about what we can't.

Ramifications Everywhere

Determining our degree of control and living with that determination has ramifications in all areas of our lives. Let's take "housecleaning" as another example. Many women who work outside the home can relate to the challenge of housecleaning when it comes to the area of partial control. I know one very successful career woman who for years found herself continually frustrated about her house not being as clean as the one she grew up in. Her mother, who did not work outside of the home, had been a very immaculate housekeeper. Her house was spotless. You could eat off the floors in her house. You couldn't find dust with a microscope in her house.

To compound the situation, this career woman married a man whose mother's house had been, if anything, even cleaner than her own mother's house. As a result, this woman felt a constant pressure to keep a clean house even though her career required that she spend her days away from home. She was frustrated, often angry, and was constantly nagging her husband and children to help her keep the house clean. She would come home from work and become a cleaning machine. She would ask the kids to pick up their things, and then she'd follow behind them picking up what they'd overlooked. In her own words, she was not "a happy camper," and everyone around her knew it.

Only when she took another look at what she was doing and the degree of control she had over the situation was she able to relieve her frustration. First, she reviewed the belief that was driving her behavior. She had a belief, she realized, on her Belief Lens that said a disorderly house meant a bad wife and mother. It was a reflection on her. So every time she saw a messy house, she transferred that to her self-worth.

But if she changed that belief to fit her lifestyle, and not her mother's or her mother-in-law's, it could meet her needs. She did just that. Her new belief became "A disorderly house means a busy family with more important things to do."

That done, her next step was accepting the fact that she only had partial control over how much picking up others would do (and less than partial control if the others happened to be teenagers). She could control her own housecleaning, of course, and her new belief actually gave her more control over herself—now that her new belief gave her new standards that didn't call for a floor clean enough to eat off of.

This woman went so far as to line up her family in the living room one night to announce that there was going to be a behavior change. The family members, as we'd all guess, were happy about the behavior change, and so was the mom. The house actually became tidier as a result, and frustration and anger went out the window. Understanding that you can't have total control over the cleanliness of your house if you're not there all the time turned out to be a very valuable realization.

Total Control

How about those things over which we have total control—such as where we're going to eat, how we want to balance our work time with our family time, or any of a hundred other things we could list? The answer is simple. If we have total control, then exercise total control. If we don't, we'll have no one to blame but ourselves. What does Nike say? Just Do It!

Let me share with you a study by Dr. Raymond Flannery of the Harvard Medical School. In his research on human behavior, Dr. Flannery found four characteristics common to what he called "stress resistant" people. The first characteristic of these enviable people was that they took charge.

If something came up, they would find a way to control it if they could. If they needed something to be fixed, they'd fix it. If they needed some information on some topic, they'd find that information. These people were in charge, in sharp contrast, Dr. Flannery found, to less stress-resistant people who would typically control almost nothing, most of the time choosing to look to others for help. Their first reaction when given an assignment was to ask as many people as possible to assist them.

The second characteristic of stress-resistant people that Dr. Flannery found was that these individuals knew what they wanted most. They had meaning and direction and purpose in their lives. Their goals were well defined, their courses well charted. These were people who were fixed on specific points and followed the paths that would get them there.

The third characteristic was a healthy lifestyle. Eighty percent of these stress-resistant people engaged in regular aerobic exercise as compared to only 20 percent of those more susceptible to stress. A healthy lifestyle also included taking time for active relaxation, on an average of ten to fifteen minutes a day. These people watched what they ate. They knew what was good for them and what wasn't.

The fourth characteristic was they had a friend, a buddy, someone they could trust and talk to, somebody they could release with, someone to share the lows and the highs with.

Incidentally, a "friend" doesn't have to necessarily be human. Having "someone to talk to" doesn't absolutely require that they talk back. Pets can be valuable tools in resisting stress. A study done by the University of Buffalo Medical School revealed that pets were more effective than spouses when it came to helping keep blood pressure and heart rate down during stressful testing.

In the study, 240 married couples were asked to perform three stressful tests, first with a spouse present, then with a dog present. Overall, physical signs of stress were highest with the spouse there. In one task that involved math problems, the study showed heartbeats rising an average of seven beats a minute higher with the dog present and thirty-seven beats a minute higher with the spouse present. Diastolic blood pressure rose eight milligrams with the dog and twenty-six milligrams with the spouse!

The study concluded that we perform better when we don't feel the pressure of evaluation—a pressure we don't get from man's (and woman's) best friend.

Being in Charge

Using the Harvard study as evidence, it seems safe to conclude that stress resistance is best realized when we make our own (calculated) choices, employ the wonders of preventive medicine, socialize effectively, and, finally, take control of our lives; and that includes control—in an interesting kind of a twist—of those things we have no control over.

Modern stress maintenance, in essence, is a process of either controlling or flowing.

Flowing is what it sounds like. When the current is too strong to do anything about it, then flow with it.

In Ugh's stone-age times, flowing wasn't really an option. The saber-toothed tiger was Ugh's obstacle, and he couldn't really go up to the tiger and say, "Hey, chill out." Ugh had two choices: fight or flight. That's the way it is with physical threats. They require a physical response. But mental threats are different. They can be dealt with through a mental response. To mental threats we can fight, flee, or flow—and flowing (some people call it "rolling with the punches") is by far the most preferable. Flowing fights fire with fire, so to speak, or mental with mental. Flowing is a response driven by a principle on a Belief Lens.

To be effective at flowing requires that we modify our beliefs, and the best way to modify our beliefs, as we've already discussed, is with self-talks. Let me suggest one self-talk—remember, self-talks are the triggers for our behavior—that I would highly encourage using in no-control situations. Simply ask yourself, "Is it worth it?" Is it worth all of the negative mental, emotional, and physical effects it's capable of causing?

He Saved Lives by Flowing

One of the great examples of "flowing" in history is Oskar Schindler. The story of this real-life Robin Hood—first told in the book and then in the Academy Award-winning movie of the same name, *Schindler's List*—is a virtual clinic in flowing.

Oskar Schindler, a Catholic-born Czechoslovakian with a penchant for business, found himself in Krakow, Poland, when Nazi Germany occupied the country and took over its affairs. Instead of fighting against these invading dictators, Schindler modified his business style so he could not only survive, but still turn a profit. Through bribes and diplomacy, he was able to get the Nazis to allow him to employ Jewish workers in his enamelware factory. This gave Schindler the manpower he needed for his factory, and it gave the Jews he employed, despite the fact that they lived in the very shadow of the Holocaust, a safe refuge.

By the time the war was over, Schindler was credited with saving the lives of 1,100 Jews, and he had maintained a successful business at the same time. At his death, he was given the "Righteous Gentile" award by the State of Israel and buried with honors in a Jerusalem cemetery.

As Oskar Schindler demonstrated, partial control over a situation can definitely be used to one's advantage as long as the boundaries are well known and well observed. Only control what you can.

Respect "No Control"

If we have absolutely no control over something, we need to respect that, too. If we get into a stress response over that something, in essence we're saying: "This is worth dying for" or at the least, "This is worth going through misery for." There are some things worth dying for, and I'm not saying there aren't. And there are some things worth getting upset or uptight or downright miserable over. But the vast majority aren't worth it. As the saying goes, "Don't sweat the small stuff—and it's all small stuff."

Often the problem is that our perception is worse than reality. We need to make sure our perceptions don't run so far away from reality that the two are on different planets, figuratively speaking; that we don't think something is worth dying for when it isn't. We can think a situation is catastrophic when in fact it is far from that. We can constantly imagine gloom and doom and pay considerably more attention to our perceptions than our realities.

Life Isn't Always Fair

Worse yet, we can allow ourselves to fall into the familiar "Life is supposed to be fair" trap. Believing that life is fair is one of the most dangerous beliefs we could ever apply to our Belief Lens. Life is not fair. On a realistic level, we all know that. We're all aware of handicaps that range from emotional to physical to economical that hit some of us harder than they hit others. Yet, if we're not careful, we can be lulled into thinking that somehow things are going to always be fair, and they won't be.

The biggest danger with a "Life is fair" belief is that the moment something unfair happens to us we are then susceptible to all the unhealthy responses. We'll be frustrated, anxious, angry, and irritable. We'll buy into all those reactions that take away our inner peace and eat away at us. But if we develop a belief on our Belief Lens that says there are unfair things that happen in life that are an integral part of existence and when they happen we'll deal with them the best we can, then we are in a position to maintain our balance and our physical, emotional, and mental health. This point was brought home to me when I was teenager and had just started to drive. I got in a minor fender bender as new drivers are wont to do, and I'll never forget coming home and having to face my dad to tell him I'd just wrecked the family car. I felt a lot of fear and trepidation as I approached my dad, anxious about what his response would be.

All my dad said was, "If you're not hurt, that's OK." He said we had insurance and not to worry about the accident, that those things happen. He taught me such a valuable lesson that day on how to respect that unfair things happen as a part of life. Sure, you want to do all you can, but sometimes, even when it's not your fault, you'll get in an accident. Those things happen.

I had a friend who got in a traffic accident and suffered whiplash. Was it fair that some young teenage driver's reckless behavior unfairly caused a lot of pain and aggravation to an innocent person? Of course it wasn't fair. But those things happen. We can either let them destroy us, or we can take them in stride as part of the process of our life and as part of the path to maximize our circumstance. Remember, as unfair things happen to you they become part of your "new" circumstances. Rather than get upset at my new circumstance, the productive response becomes, "What can I do to maximize my new circumstance."

Looking at Assets

One of the best ways to keep perception and reality in close proximity is to keep a firm grip on our individual assets. Taking a regular inventory of the positive things in our lives can be one of the best hedges against runaway fears and worries. A good way to take mental inventory is to create safety deposit boxes in our minds—to dwell on the things that are fair. At least for us.

I knew of a man who was very wealthy and very successful, but who was nonetheless constantly worried about how well the current project he was working on would turn out and, after that project was concluded, about what he would work on next. What if another project didn't come along? What if this current project was a bust? What if and what if and what if? He was a walking, talking, negative time bomb. Anxiety was a constant companion. They went everywhere together. He fretted and worried all the time. He paid virtually no attention to the fact that during an already lengthy career he had piled up one success after another and was the envy of those around him. He was very talented and accomplished.

This man had access to a very positive resource that for much of his life he chose to ignore. That positive resource was his mental safety deposit box. Once he realized it was there and started paying regular visits, through self-talks, it produced exceptional dividends. Those visits revealed treasures he had kept well hidden from himself, treasures of great worth.

In his safety deposit box, he discovered he had more than enough money to take care of himself and his loved ones the rest of their lives, whether any additional money came in or not. He discovered he'd already been successful at any number of projects, and those could never be taken away. What's more, he realized he'd always had enough projects to keep him as busy as he wanted to be, so why should that change now?

Once he became familiar with the whereabouts of his personal safety deposit box, he got in the habit of visiting it often. Whenever those old negative thoughts of failure and insecurity arose, he would take a trip to visit his assets.

Take Inventory

You can likewise take your own inventory. See how many assets you can come up with. Remember that this is not just a financial safety deposit box. This is for all of the four needs: live, love, self-esteem, and enjoy. Some questions that might help you identify your inventory include:

- What financial assets do I have should my current circumstances change?

- What skills do I have?

- What accomplishments am I particularly proud of?

- What personality traits really help me get through the bad times?

- What do I like about myself?

- What relationships make me feel good?

- Where are my safe places?

- What are my favorite things to do or share?

- Where would I like to be, with whom, and doing what on an ideal weekend?

- What kinds of risks do I most often take?

Put these answers in your safety deposit box and add anything else you can think of. How about pets? Your church? If you consider such things as assets in your life, put them in. If you have a close personal friend, a best buddy, that's a definite asset. Anything that makes you feel better about yourself or helps you in your life should be in your safety deposit box. A good sense of humor should definitely be listed as a valuable asset. What hobbies keep you interested in life? Find a spot for them in your box of assets.

Once you've taken your inventory, determine that you will go through this mental exercise on a regular basis. It's a most effective way for us to take positive stock of our lives. It's all based on reality. The more we put into our safety deposit boxes, the less threatening those things we have little or no control over become. Imagining unfortunate events, such as being laid off from work or having to move, will become less threatening as we realize our stock of assets is sufficient to carry us through tough times.

The more we visit our mental safety deposit boxes, the better we'll think of ourselves and the more secure we'll feel. It can give us the kind of security that allows us to get outside of ourselves and help others who we might perceive as less fortunate. The average American has two clinically diagnosed episodes of depression between ages thirty-five and sixty-five.

One of the best ways to treat depression is to help someone less fortunate than yourself. You can always find someone worse off. By helping them you feel better about yourself, you boost your self-esteem, and hence treat your own depression.

Taking a mental inventory can also help us identify those assets we don't have but would like to achieve. Once we feel comfortable that we are in control of a number of assets, adding to our "stash" will become easier and easier. We'll consider ourselves both wealthy and secure.

We'll feel in control.

Instant Replay

Key Points

- It's as important to know what we can't control as what we can.

- Life is not fair. When unfair things happen to us they become part of our new circumstance.

- Events over which we have no control require us to flow.

- We flow by modifying beliefs on our Belief Lens.

- We all have mental safety deposit boxes filled with our assets.

- Our assets in our mental safety deposit boxes determine if the threats in our lives are real or perceived.

Personal Exercise

- Fill in the control continuum to identify how much control you have over the obstacles in your life.

- Create a safety deposit box of your assets in your four need areas to identify if the threats in your life are real or perceived.

Where Do We Go from Here?

In chapter ten, we'll discuss moving our lives past being successful to having true significance.

CHAPTER TEN

FROM SUCCESS TO SIGNIFICANCE

We spend a large portion of our lives looking for a way to become successful, yet when we get there, we discover that we're still looking for a way to add meaning and significance to our lives.

Money can buy you happiness. No, that's not a type-o. Money can, indeed, buy you happiness—depending on how you spend it. A Gallup survey conducted in 153 countries, known as "The World Giving Index 2010," revealed that there was more of a correlation between a country's degree of happiness and giving than between its wealth and giving. What does that mean? Those countries that gave more money away than what they kept for themselves were happier. We've been conditioned to think that accumulating great wealth leads to happiness, yet this study shows that even poor countries that give more to charities report higher levels of happiness than those nations that are much wealthier yet have lower levels of charitable giving.

In a speech given at a TED conference, Michael Norton, a Harvard Business School associate professor, cited the World Giving Index and stated, "If you think money can't buy happiness, you're not spending it right. You should stop thinking about which product to buy for yourself and try giving some of it to other people instead." Norton continued, citing another study that reported a connection between charitable giving and happiness, explaining, "people who spent money on other people got happier; people who spent money on themselves, nothing happened. It didn't make them less happy; it just didn't do much for them."

A study conducted at the University of British Columbia backs up this notion shared by Norton. The study involved groups of students who were given money to spend either on themselves or on others. Those that spent the money on others reported greater happiness than those who spent the money on themselves.

So, can money actually buy happiness? It really does come down to how you spend it. Research indicates that when you spend money on others or participate in charitable giving—even if you live in poverty—your happiness will increase. However, accumulating things or living a fun and luxurious lifestyle seems to have a tendency of creating a spiraling descent into despair and addiction, even as people conduct a constant search for the next new purchase or activity that will fill the void of happiness in their lives. We've seen that scenario play out time and again in the lives of the "rich and famous."

Not a New Idea

Let's return to our retired executives that were introduced in chapter one. These executives were all very successful, yet their responses to the study's questions reveal that they were looking for more than just success in life; they were looking for significance.

Of course, this search for significance beyond professional and even personal success isn't new. We've all heard from our earliest days—despite the first line of this chapter—that money, fame, or any other type of success do not necessarily bring happiness. The major flaw in the idea that money or fame can bring you happiness is that it is primarily "me-centric." In this me-centric approach to happiness, the entire focus is on me: my needs, my desires, my priorities, my happiness. Me, me, me. We never branch out or expand our circle of concern. Ultimately, when we stop to look back at our lives, we find that we are alone in those circles, lacking not only company but also meaning and purpose. In terms of our discussion, the belief that happiness can be found through me-centric pursuits is a hindering belief. We tell ourselves that once we are rich, famous, or successful, we'll be happy, and then we're blindsided by the realization that our lives are still missing something.

On the flip side of that argument lays the "you-centric" approach. A you-centric approach focuses on the needs of others. I'm not saying that you shouldn't do things that are important to you, or that you shouldn't work to become successful. Improving yourself and your station in life is a worthwhile endeavor. Just remember that once you reach the top, the view is much better when you have someone to share it with.

The Community Commerce model, as presented by MonaVie, teaches that success is achieved as you help others become successful. This is another instance where this idea and what the world teaches don't exactly mesh. We live in a competitive world; we're trained to believe that in order for there to be a winner, there must also be a loser. I can tell you, if I had stopped to help my fellow racers, I would never have set any records or competed in the Olympics. Yet, despite my experiences on the track, I've personally seen how ensuring the success of others helps ensure your own success. It sounds counterintuitive, but it works and we'll look at why.

This you-centric approach is an empowering belief. Given that we've already established that empowering beliefs are largely determined by putting beliefs to test and then viewing the results through the lens of experience, how can I state that a you-centric approach to life is an empowering belief? Because it has been proven time and time again to be a belief that empowers people to do and be more. In fact, one of the activities that those successful executives we've been talking about said that they would do if they could do it all again was to provide more service.

Its Own Reward

Believe it or not, our bodies are actually hardwired to think of the welfare of others. When we act altruistically, our bodies release oxytocin. Oxytocin is one of the "feel good" hormones and is often referred to as the "compassion hormone." Acts of service, even small acts of kindness, trigger the release of oxytocin, creating an instant physiological reward. Service, then, is a natural tendency and one that has been with mankind since our earliest days.

This idea flies in the face of our belief that we are programmed for self-preservation. If both Ugh and Doug were confronted by the tiger, a self-preservation program would dictate that all Ugh needs to do is just run faster than Doug—natural selection strikes again; sacrifice the weak to preserve the strong (or the fleet of foot). But what we've just been discussing is that Ugh would receive a greater reward not just spiritually but physiologically if he were to stay and help Doug escape as well.

Given that altruism is a part of our nature, is it any wonder that the idea of caring for the welfare of others pops up in nearly every religion, philosophy, or belief system? All the greatest teachers and leaders throughout history have taught the simple idea that giving service is the surest way to find significance in your life. Most Christians will recognize these words from Jesus: "Whosoever shall seek his life shall lose it; and whosoever shall lose his life shall preserve it" (Luke 17:33). Confucius, the ancient Chinese philosopher, shared the same idea in this way: "A man of humanity is one who, in seeking to establish himself, finds a foothold for others and who, desiring attainment for himself, helps others to attain." Mahatma Gandhi put it even more succinctly, stating, "The best way to find yourself is to lose yourself in service to others."

Let's adapt those words into our next Natural Law:

When we focus our life on our own desires, our lives become less significant; but, when we spend our time helping others, we find greater meaning and purpose.

Service brings out the best in each of us, and I'm not just talking about socially. Service improves several areas of our lives, even meeting the needs in our Needs Quadrants. "Research has revealed an interesting link between helping others and enjoying a good quality of life," explains Professor Paul Whitely of the University of Essex, who conducted a study on service at a community level. "It seems that when we focus on the needs of others, we may also reap benefits ourselves. It means that voluntary activity in the community is associated with better health, lower crime, improved educational performance, and greater life satisfaction."

A study supported by Simplyhealth and conducted by Mindlab International found that altruism caused the following in their study group:

- An average increase in self-esteem by 31 percent

- Stress levels lowered by 36 percent

- Feelings of anger reduced

- An increase in positive thoughts and feelings

According to the study, concerning ourselves with the needs of others has a direct effect on our self-esteem need (a 31 percent improvement in how we view ourselves). A reduction in feelings of anger can only help to meet our need to love, while positive thoughts and feelings help us to enjoy life that much more. And let's not underestimate the 36 percent reduction in stress levels. With all the negative effects of stress on our health (increased blood pressure, lack of sleep, diminished immune system, etc.), the promise that providing service to others lowers stress levels definitely gives us a step up in meeting our need to live.

Additional studies have found that there is even a reported decrease in aches and pains among those who provide service. According to a survey of 4,000 adults conducted by UnitedHealthcare and VolunteerMatch, 68 percent of participants felt better physically after starting to volunteer and just under 30 percent stated that volunteering was helping them manage a chronic condition. Stephen Post, author of *Why Good Things Happen to Good People* and director of the Center for Medical Humanities, Compassionate Care, and Bioethics at Stony Brook University, promised that "one of the best ways to get your mind off your aches and pains is to get your mind onto somebody else."

Happiness through service even appears to be a self-perpetuating cycle. A study out of Japan by Keiko Otaki, found that happy people were more likely to do small acts of kindness and that by doing so they increased their own happiness even more. In other words, doing good makes us want to do more good, which makes us feel happier and leads to doing more good—an honest-to-goodness beneficial addiction. The same study reported that listing out the acts of kindness performed during the course of a week had a positive effect on happiness levels, which is an interesting activity that you can do on your own at any time.

Here's a question for you: How did you feel the last time you heard someone tell a story about service? I'd be willing to bet that you felt happier, and I have the science to back up that assumption. Another interesting study reported that just hearing about someone else's good deeds increases mood and desires to go out and do service. For that matter, how have you felt as you have been reading about service in this chapter? Again, I'll bet you feel pretty good. A 1988 study out of Harvard coined the term the "Mother Teresa Effect." Students were shown a film of Mother Teresa caring for orphans in Calcutta and then tested for a salivary immunoglobulin—a protective antibody and a part of your immune system. The study found that students who watched the film experienced an uptick in this immunoglobulin. In other words, just thinking about service has a positive effect on your body's immune system.

It's in our nature to help others. When we do, our minds and bodies respond positively, reducing stress and improving mood. Doing good really is its own reward.

The Man in the Mirror

If a you-centric approach to life is so wonderful, then why don't we serve more? It comes down to our Belief Lens.

What are the beliefs on your lens? Are they beliefs that point you toward others? Me-centric beliefs not only keep us from serving and giving, they also obscure our Belief Lens. In effect, a me-centric approach transforms our Belief Lenses into belief mirrors.

Mirrors have been around for thousands of years, but the modern method of making a mirror is insightful to our discussion. Modern mirrors are created through a process of "silvering" one side of a clear piece of glass. Through this process, layers are added to the back of a piece of glass creating the reflective surface. These layers generally start with a liquefied tin, which is applied because the next layer—silver or aluminum—won't stick to the glass. After the silver is applied, a layer of copper is added, followed by a sealant and then two layers of paint. In other words, blocking out one side of what would otherwise be a transparent lens creates mirrors.

Living a me-centric lifestyle has much the same effect on our Belief Lenses. Me-centric beliefs reflect our attention back on ourselves. This lifestyle "silvers" the outside of our lenses, adding layers of hindering beliefs that block out our view until we are left only being able to see ourselves.

The classic story of Narcissus and Echo portrays the danger of silvering our lenses. Narcissus was a young hunter who was well known for being very handsome. Unfortunately, Narcissus was all too aware of his own beauty, (hence the word "narcissistic"). One day while hunting, Narcissus discovered a pool of water and, as Ovid explains in Book III of the *Metamorphoses*, Narcissus is "captivated by the image of beauty he has seen" and he falls deeply in love with "all the things for which he himself is admired." While Narcissus is caught in this state, the nymph Echo tries vainly to express her love to him. But, because of a curse, she can only repeat back the words someone else has already spoken. Eventually, both Echo and Narcissus waste away, neither ever enjoying true love.

When our Belief Lenses become belief mirrors, we become captivated with our own reflection. Eventually, aspects of our character and abilities that we possess waste away while we focus only on what we can see in the mirror. Even more tragic, while we are caught in the virtual life presented by our mirrors, those around us suffer from our lack of attention. Our ability to view their needs is blocked by our own me-centric beliefs. In the end, our opportunity for love and significance is lost in a reflection of what life is.

What Narcissus—and narcissistic people in general—missed out on is discovering what true beauty is. Psychologists from the University of Liverpool conducted a number of experiments on people's understanding of mirrors. In one experiment, study participants were asked to walk along a line parallel to a partially covered mirror. They were then asked to guess at what point they would be able to see their own reflection. What the researchers discovered was that the participants grossly overestimated when they would be able to see their reflection. The participants felt that they could see themselves before even getting to a point where they were level with the near edge of the mirror.

Dr. Marco Bertamini, a member of the team of psychologists conducting the experiments, explained, "People tend not to understand that the location of the viewer matters in terms of what is visible in a mirror. A good example of this is what we call the Venus Effect, which relates to the many famous paintings of the goddess Venus looking in a small mirror." Now here is the crux of Dr. Bertamini's explanation: "If you were to look at these paintings, you would assume that Venus is admiring her own face, because you see her face in the mirror. Your viewpoint, however, is rather different from hers; if you can see her in the mirror then she would see you in the mirror."

The more we come to understand empowering beliefs, the more we see that those beliefs push us beyond our own narrow view of the world. They expand our horizons by refocusing our attention onto others. Just as Venus, the goddess of beauty—and love!—reveals in her view of the mirror, true, inner beauty is discovered when we change our view to include others.

Changing our view may require us to reverse the "silvering" process on our Belief Lenses. A mirror can be returned to its transparent state by scraping off the silvering on the back. Like most bad habits, the process is not easy. While it is too simple to turn our lenses into mirrors, the reversal process takes work as you scrape of layers of beliefs that have blocked your view. But, again, like most things, the harder the work, the greater the reward. Clearing our Belief Lenses of "silvering" beliefs opens our view to a new world—a world that we've been missing out on while we've focused on ourselves.

Creating Significance

When you look at history in terms of moving from success to significance, you start to see a common thread of altruism in those people that we celebrate for their goodness. In fact, take a moment and do just that. Set down this book and make a list of the people throughout all of history that you admire the most. What made them great? What made them stand out from the rest of the pack? Certainly they were successful in what they did; no doubt you could make a long list of people who are famous for excelling at something, but did those people make your list of people that you admire? Or are the people on your admired list those who found true significance that came from a you-centric approach to life?

The secret that these successful people discovered is available for each of us to apply in our own lives as well. Now, I'm not saying that each of us will have a chapter dedicated to our lives in the history books of the future. I am saying that we can move from success to significance in our own lives through thinking of others first. Greater purpose and meaning in your life is waiting to be discovered.

Just as our Natural Law suggests, the more you give of yourself, the more you'll find to give. It's one of the great mysteries of life that isn't really that mysterious. When you focus on helping others to be happy, you find happiness. Those that give tend to have more to give—both in terms of time and finances. Don't believe me? Then put it to the test. Develop a genuine and sincere desire to help someone and see if the rewards don't overcompensate for the little you do give. I think you'll be surprised by the results. I know I have been.

Giving More

Service and giving of yourself is one of the major tenets of my own beliefs, and I've tried to always live my life in such a fashion that I can give. That's why, when I began working with the other founders of MonaVie, we sought out a worthy charity to help support.

Our search led us to the *favelas*, or slums, of Rio de Janeiro. One in five people that live in Rio live in the *favelas*. With a population over six million, that's a lot of people that are living in debilitating poverty. The saddest part of this statistic is that 12 percent of the children in Brazil live on the streets, creating a self-perpetuating cycle of poverty that few escape from. These families and children have little hope of ever escaping the daily grind of making enough money to simply survive that day.

One person who has worked tirelessly to overcome this escalating social ill is Sergio Ponce. Sergio grew up in Rio, playing with the children in the *favelas*. As an adult, Sergio found himself returning to the *favelas* in search of ways to help. Unfortunately, Sergio discovered that, despite his good intentions, lack of funding, resources, and volunteers hindered his ability to help where help was needed most. That's where MonaVie came in.

Because each of the MonaVie founders, myself included, subscribe to the empowering belief that serving others leads to true significance, we decided early on that we would give back, especially to the country that gave us the açaí berry (the main ingredient in MonaVie products). With Sergio's help, we launched the MORE Project.

The MORE Project's main focus is providing opportunities, resources, and assistance to families and children. Resources are given to provide children with healthy meals. Homes are built and repaired by the MORE Project. Perhaps even more important, the MORE Project provides educational opportunities, which translates into better employment and advancement opportunities. Finally, the MORE Project also provides medical care, including a dedicated psychologist, to help children and their parents to have healthier, happier lives. The MORE Project started with the families and children of the *favelas* in Rio, but has expanded to include projects in Thailand and India with plans to expand even more.

Perhaps the most interesting aspect of the MORE Project has been the opportunity to be a personal witness to the generosity of thousands of people. The MORE Project has been a bit of an experiential laboratory where I've seen this belief of finding significance through service put to the test. The MORE Project, while funded by MonaVie, receives the majority of its resources through the generosity of MonaVie distributors—independent contractors who sell MonaVie products through the Community Commerce business model

I've watched as these distributors have opened their hearts and wallets to help those in need. I've traveled to Brazil with groups of distributors who have given of their time to help families and children. Beyond that, I've witnessed the positive changing effect that this service has had on these people. Many of these distributors are wildly successful, yet when they talk about the things that they are most proud of, they talk about how they have been able to help others—often listing their involvement with the MORE Project as one of those ways. They may have found success in their work, but they discovered significance in their giving.

The Good News

The good news about all of this is that you can find the same level of significance in your own life. It doesn't take much. As I've already mentioned, you may not make it into the history books, but you don't have to in order to have a satisfying and significant life.

Moving from success to significance can start with even the most simple of acts. How many times throughout any given day do you have the opportunity to open a door, give a supportive word, help lighten someone's heavy load, or put an arm of comfort around someone who is struggling? Your mind and body don't distinguish between small and random acts of kindness and million dollar donations. You'll still experience the release of oxytocin; you'll still feel better about yourself; you'll still see greater meaning and purpose in your life.

From these small random acts, you can build up to larger, more planned acts of service. Start in you neighborhood. Do you have a neighbor that could use some help? What about your community—are there opportunities to serve where you live? There are so many worthy causes out there—the MORE Project being one of them—that finding opportunities to serve is simple. Start by finding a cause close to your heart; something that you feel passionate about. Once you have decided on what your cause is, search out ways in which you can help. While every organization will gladly accept monetary donations, many are also starving for volunteers to donate their time and energy to the cause. Whether you give time or money, do so regularly.

Then, as we've been discussing, analyze your service through your Belief Lens. Did the behavior meet a need—self-esteem, love, live, or enjoy?

Remember, an empowering belief will drive behavior that satisfies needs over time; hindering beliefs drive behavior that does not satisfactorily meet our needs. As you serve others, are you meeting your needs? If so, then service would be an empowering belief for you. If your actions are not meeting your needs, then you may have more work to do to change your belief mirror back into a Belief Lens.

As you go about defining what is on your Belief Lens, make sure to reserve space for this belief. When you do, you'll find the significance you're looking for. Perhaps one of the greatest examples of a person who not only has service as a belief on his lens, but whose lens is primarily defined by service, is the Dalai Lama. In speaking of his beliefs, the Dalai Lama explained, "My religion is very simple. My religion is kindness." Adopt the same religion and you'll find the significance you're searching for.

Instant Replay

Key Points

- A me-centric approach to life will leave you feeling empty, even if you reach the top. Exchanging that approach for a you-centric one creates a life filled with greater significance.

- Doing good is a natural part of our being. When we do good, our bodies respond with "feel good" hormones and improvements in our overall health and outlook.

- When we focus on ourselves, we can actually transform our Belief Lenses into belief mirrors, which ultimately robs us of any chance at discovering true significance.

- Through service—big or small—we create more significance.

Personal Exercise

• Identify a cause that you feel passionate about. Volunteer your time or donate to it.

• Explore your feelings after donating. How do you feel about yourself? Did your donation help meet any of your needs? Would your experience lead you to accepting service as an empowering belief? Why?

Where Do We Go from Here?

In chapter eleven, we'll learn about a powerful tool we call the "Why Drill." Its purpose is to help us drill to the core of what's driving our behavior.

CHAPTER ELEVEN

WHY ASK WHY?

When we were kids, we never stopped with the questions; so why stop now? Asking why we behave a certain way can help us identify the beliefs that are driving us.

Children can be terrific role models in demonstrating how to deal with life. One thing that children do particularly well is ask, "Why?" Why does it rain? Why does the sun come up in the east and go down in the west? Why do bees sting? Why do I have to go to bed?

We all used the "Why Drill" extensively as children. The reason was simple: The "Why Drill" gave us answers. It was how we learned. As we grow up we tend to put it on a shelf and not use it very often, which is too bad. Effective use of the "Why Drill" allows us to probe to the very core of what motivates and drives us. The "Why Drill" is a most effective way to uncover our personal truths and beliefs and help us answer whether they empower us or not.

The "Why Drill"

The need to use the "Why Drill" becomes quickly obvious once we put it into practice. Too often the results of our behavior go unchecked. We become creatures of habit. We do something today because that's what we did yesterday. We don't ask for answers like we did when we were children. Even when we're struggling, instead of questioning, we tend to continue with the same repetitive behavior. The "Why Drill" is valuable because it helps us identify why we're struggling by identifying hindering beliefs. Remember, the definition of a hindering belief is something that drives behavior that does not meet my needs over time. The first step to achieving our personal best is a clear identification of our hindering beliefs—those beliefs on our Belief Lens that trigger behavior and results that don't meet our needs over time. Once we clearly identify hindering beliefs, we're in a position to replace them with empowering beliefs that do meet our needs over time.

The "Why Drill" is easy to use. There's no electricity necessary or any other power source beyond our own minds. If we simply start asking "why," we're instantly operational. We turn on the "Why Drill" simply by asking "why" questions about our behavior.

My Own Experience

Let me use my own life's experience as an example. In earlier chapters, I've already related my experiences as a lawyer and how I eventually left the practice of law because I determined it was not fulfilling my needs. It took a long time for me to make that change; and remember, that change didn't occur until the pain was great enough for me to do something about it. If I had known about the "Why Drill" and used it effectively, I could have saved myself a lot of that pain.

I have often asked people to go ahead and ask me any "why" questions they want about my behavior as a lawyer to identify the belief on my Belief Lens and the need behind it that was driving my behavior.

Usually the first question asked is "Why did you choose law?"

"Well," I would answer, "I chose law because I remember a distinct feeling from a very early age that if I was going to be looked up to when I got older, if I was going to be somebody important, I should be a doctor or a lawyer. Since there was a long tradition of law in my family, I chose lawyer over doctor."

The next "Why Drill" question was always something like, "Why did you think being a lawyer or a doctor would make you important?"

My answer: "Because that's what people constantly told me. 'I hope you grow up to be a lawyer or doctor,' they'd say. Over and over again, I heard about the esteemed status of lawyers. If I was a lawyer, I would be respected, and people would think well of me." This was reinforced every time I observed someone meeting another person. They would introduce themselves, and then ask what they did for a living. As soon as they told them what they did, they were immediately categorized. I could see this. I learned that people think more highly of you if you're in a "prestige" profession.

Often it will take more than two "why" questions to get to the belief on a Belief Lens that drives behavior. But in this example, that's all it took. After hearing my response to just two questions, it's safe to conclude the following:

- I chose to practice law because the belief on my Belief Lens is that others' perception of my job determines my self-worth.

- The need threatened is my self-esteem need.

The belief on my Belief Lens goes way back to when I was a child—and an avid practitioner, I should add, of the "Why Drill."

It was the same with my early introduction to athletics. By employing the "Why Drill" it's not difficult to see why I shaped a belief on my Belief Lens that beating other people was necessary for me to satisfy my self-esteem need. Almost from the first time I participated in sports, that belief was reinforced. Every time I'd come back from a race, what would people ask me? They'd ask me how I did. "Did you win?" If I said I did win they'd say, "Yeah, all right. Good job. Way to go. We're proud of you." On the other hand, if I said I lost, they'd get a sympathetic look on their faces and say, "Oh, that's too bad! Better luck next time."

So winning is important, that's what I kept hearing. And what's winning? It's beating other people. You can't win and not beat other people. It's all relative. Success, praise, fame, and fortune are contingent upon finishing higher than other people. If that's what I believe, then that's what's on my Belief Lens. And, that's what will drive my behavior as I strive to satisfy my self-esteem need.

When the "Why Drill" question is why do I feel winning is important, that's my answer. That's why.

Apply the Natural Laws

The "Why Drill" wouldn't do us much good if we stopped here. Only when we apply important Natural Laws, or values, does it help us shape new beliefs to drive behavior that will result in change in our lives. In the case of the self-esteem need—and that's the one that applies to my two personal examples I have given—I discovered the Natural Law to be this:

When my self-esteem is dependent on something external, I will not meet my needs over time.

By "external" I mean, of course, anything outside my control. If I have a need dependent on something outside my control, that's going to leave me, sooner or later, out of control. And if I'm out of control, more often than not, I'm going to be frustrated, anxious, and incapable of making decisions—a reactor rather than a pro-actor.

If my self-esteem is dependent on something internal, then that changes everything because now I'm in control. I'm in charge. If something's frustrating me or making me anxious, it's within my power to change it. That makes all the difference in the world.

Again, using my personal examples with the law and athletics, my two original beliefs were based on things external. I believed I was only as important as how others perceived my profession. And I believed winning is beating other people. Both beliefs relied on other people's perceptions and behavior, not mine. Only when I changed to internal beliefs in both cases—that my profession was important if it was enjoyable and fulfilling to me and that winning meant giving my best shot—was I able to have behavior driven by empowering beliefs that met my self-esteem need over time.

By using the "Why Drill," that becomes clear.

Why Drill Example

Let's look at an example of how you might conduct a Why Drill. Let's say that you're experiencing trouble getting people out to your home reviews. You routinely invite ten or more people to the meeting, and you always make sure to get promises from attendees that they will be there. Yet, your record high attendance is only two! This causes you to feel insecure and anxious, which you don't like. You don't want to feel insecure, and all the anxiety is really wearing you out. You would much rather feel calm, confident, and at peace. But you don't have that.

So let's apply the "Why Drill" to the situation.

FIRST QUESTION: "WHY DOES IT STRESS YOU OUT WHEN NO ONE COMES TO YOUR HOME REVIEW?"

Answer: *Because if no one comes to my home reviews, then I'll never make a sale or recruit anyone.*

SECOND QUESTION: "WHY DOES IT MATTER TO YOU IF YOU NEVER MAKE A SALE OR RECRUIT ANYONE?"

Answer: *Because if I never sell anything or add to my organization, I'll never progress through the ranks and earn more money.*

THIRD QUESTION: "WHY DO YOU HAVE ANXIETY ABOUT PROGRESSING THROUGH THE RANKS AND EARNING MORE MONEY?"

Answer: *Because building a successful business is key to my being able to achieve my dreams and goals.*

FOURTH QUESTION: "WHY IS BUILDING A SUCCESSFUL BUSINESS
SO IMPORTANT TO YOUR DREAMS AND
GOALS?"

Answer: *Because without the income that a successful business provides, I won't be able to achieve those dreams and goals.*

FIFTH QUESTION: "AND WHY DO YOU NEED THE INCOME OF A
SUCCESSFUL BUSINESS?"

Answer: *Because it will allow me to provide for myself and my family and because it contributes to my feelings of self-worth.*

From these questions and answers, the "Why Drill" cuts to the heart of your belief that says "When no one shows up to my meetings, I won't be able to provide for myself and my family." That being your belief, it's going to drive behavior that produces anxiety, insecurity, and confusion every time no one shows up for your home review. Since that kind of behavior produces results that do not meet your needs over time (your self-esteem need will definitely be adversely affected and your insecure behavior could drive you right out of the opportunity that's paramount in satisfying your need to live), you're now in position to look at the hindering belief and change it to an empowering belief. After you understand the "why," you can implement the change.

In our hypothetical case involving attendance at your home meetings, you'd want to change your belief from your initial external outlook (low attendance means I will fail) to an internal belief that would give you control.

First, assess what you don't have control over. In this case, you don't have control over people's attendance at your home review. If they promise you that they will attend and then change their minds, then that is their prerogative. That being a given, you need to look at what beliefs will drive internal control. You need to come up with a new belief that, instead of generating an unhealthy response to something over which you have no control, will empower you to generate a healthy response to something you can control.

You need to realize that the situation, whatever it is, will happen again; and when it does, it will be much more beneficial for you to be able to generate a different, healthy response.

Theoretical New Belief Comes First

The first step is to come up with a theoretical new belief that when strongly imprinted will drive the behavior and responses that are really wanted and will meet your needs over time. Ask yourself, "What new theoretical belief can I live by that will drive new responses that will empower me to flow in a situation over which I have no control?" The reality of actually implementing this theoretical new belief will come later, and we'll discuss how to do that in detail in the next chapter. But first, it's important to realize that the first step is to identify the theoretical new beliefs and firmly imprint them.

Continuing with our example of dealing with a fear of no one attending your home review meetings, how about a theoretical new belief that "Every home review that I hold is an opportunity to practice and hone my skills. Regardless of who is in attendance—even if no one is in attendance—I'm going to give my best presentation because practice will only improve my performance when I do have large groups"? Both are internal. Both turn the low attendance at your meetings into a positive instead of a negative. How about this new theoretical belief on your Belief Lens: "If I always do my best and keep working at the things that have made others successful, I will be successful too"?

Will that make low attendance at your home business reviews less anxious and threatening? Of course it will. Even though nothing external will have changed, you will have changed (by modifying a belief on your Belief Lens).

Along the way, of course, we'll also become a lot more tolerant of those around us. That's inherent with behavior that is inward looking and not outward looking. If we're not always telling people what they should be, narrow-mindedness will change to broad-mindedness. Expectations that we thrust onto others often set us up for disappointment. That doesn't mean we should approve or excuse rude behavior by other people. It means we should give other people enough space to allow them their own opinions and decisions. Appreciating the differences in others brings about workable, complementary solutions instead of adversarial relationships. All this is a byproduct of inward-oriented behavior driven by internal beliefs. In other words, by looking inside we become our own best allies and not our own worst enemies.

Think Before You Leap

There's a story I read in the newspaper a few years ago that I think illustrates this point very well, and very soberly. It involved a basketball player who was trying to make the roster of an NBA team. The player was a center, close to seven feet tall, and, like all those invited to try out for the team, had been a star in college. He survived the early cuts and made it onto the team that would play in the exhibition season that preceded the regular season. He was very close to realizing his lifelong dream of playing professional basketball in the NBA.

When the team took its first road trip of the exhibition season, a problem arose. On the flight to the game, this player was assigned a seat in the coach cabin while the veteran players and several of the team's coaches and administrators sat in the first class cabin. As he sat in his coach seat, which had considerably less leg room than his seven-foot frame needed, the player got more and more frustrated. Adding to his frustration was the fact that the team's general manager was one of those he'd seen sitting in first class. He knew there was a rule in the standard NBA player's contract that said players were supposed to get airplane seat priority over noncoaches, and that included the general manager.

When the plane landed the player had had sufficient time to get incensed enough that he complained to the general manager over the inequity of the seating arrangements. He told him he wasn't happy about being treated unfairly and that on the return flight he expected that he and the general manager would switch seats. He'd be in first class and the general manager would be in coach.

You can probably guess what happened next.

The general manager told the player he could fly back in whatever seat he liked because as of right this moment he could consider himself no longer a member of the team!

There is no question that the aspiring NBA player was right in his interpretation of the rules. But he missed one key point. He wasn't on the team yet. He lost track of what he had control over and what he didn't have control over. This was a classic case of sacrificing what was wanted most (an NBA career) for what was wanted now (more leg room). If the college star had brought out the "Why Drill" as he sat in his coach seat instead of negative self-talks, he'd have played in that night's game and perhaps the next game and the one after that, until he was a full-fledged member of the team. Instead of brooding over what he perceived as mistreatment, he'd have first asked himself, "Why are you upset?" Before long he'd have concluded that the belief on his Belief Lens was that he was a star, he'd always been a star (in junior high, high school, and college), and if he wasn't being treated like a star he wasn't respected. Armed with that knowledge, he'd have been able to reason that a better theoretical belief in his rather precarious situation would be something like, "I'm a rookie now, and all rookies, no matter who they are and how great they were in college, have to go through boot camp. Being treated like a rookie means I'm on the first step to a lengthy and satisfying career as an NBA basketball player."

He'd have gotten off the plane smiling as the circulation returned to his legs, and he'd have asked the general manager if he'd had a nice flight.

Exercise Principles

Let's look at another example. Let's say that you hate to exercise. Exercise for you is completely unpleasurable. You'd rather sit through the Ice Follies than exercise.

First, apply the "Why Drill."

FIRST QUESTION: "WHY DO YOU HATE TO EXERCISE?"
Answer: *Because it's no fun.*

SECOND QUESTION: "WHY IS IT NO FUN?"
Answer: *Because it's boring, it takes too much time, and I don't get anything out of it.*

THIRD QUESTION: "WHY DON'T YOU FEEL LIKE YOU GET ANYTHING OUT OF IT?"
Answer: *Because it takes me away from the things I really enjoy doing.*

Notice that in this "Why Drill" example the questions and answers are going in a circle. Before long, we'd be right back to the question "Why do you hate to exercise?" and the answer "Because it's no fun." That brings us, in a roundabout way, to the conclusion that you have a belief on your Belief Lens that says either exercise should be enjoyable or everything you do in your spare time should be fun and enjoyable. Somewhere in your life, you've picked up that belief. Perhaps from the ads on TV for exercise equipment that feature smiling, fit models who act as if they're having the time of their lives (and never sweat). Or perhaps from friends who have talked glowingly of their "exercise highs." Or perhaps from a notion that you work hard when you're on the job and everything else you do in life is your reward for that hard work, and exercise is not a reward. You don't choose to spend your free time in pain.

Whatever its origin, you have that belief—that exercise should be fun—and since every time you've tried to exercise you've found it no fun, you don't keep doing it, you have bad results, and the needs you're trying to meet aren't being met.

Once you understand "why," however, you're ready for a new theoretical belief, which might be along the lines of "The primary reason for exercise isn't to have fun, it's to take care of my body so I'll feel better, look better, and have more energy for the important things in my life." Or maybe "Exercise only becomes fun after I'm in sufficient shape to enjoy it."

To reinforce that new theoretical belief you might think about other examples of things you do, or have done, in your life that aren't necessarily "fun" but are still eminently worthwhile—studying for a test in school, for example, or growing a garden. Those are things that take work before they yield results. As it is with these things, so it is with exercise.

Armed with that new theoretical belief, you can imagine jumping on your stationary bike, your rowing machine, or your cross-country ski simulator and grinning and bearing the pain as you physically exert. Your new theoretical belief will trigger new visualized behavior, which in turn will generate results that will meet your needs. Again, in the following chapter we will discuss how to turn our theoretical beliefs into reality.

Always Add the Words "Over Time"

In any example we choose to use, remember that we have to add the words "over time" to our final analysis. Will the theoretical belief on my Belief Lens drive behavior that will meet my needs over time? When the answer is in the affirmative, we know we have a theoretical belief that can empower us.

The beauty of the "Why Drill" is that it can be used in all situations of our lives to help us focus on the beliefs that drive our behavior. Sometimes it can take a while to get to the belief, and sometimes the belief is quickly recognizable. Whatever the case, it's the accurate appraisal of that belief that frees us to change. We can't really find out anything until we start asking questions.

Besides working for us as individuals, the "Why Drill" can also be used effectively as we look at others we associate with—as was the case with the aspiring NBA basketball player—as well as situations in general in our lives.

For example, if we have a downline or sideline who has a certain style of doing things and that style doesn't exactly jibe with our style of doing things, exercising the "Why Drill" can help us understand the beliefs on our downline's or sideline's Belief Lens that are driving his or her behavior. We can ask the "why" questions either silently to ourselves or directly to the other person with sensitivity and diplomacy. There is great value that comes from understanding other people's beliefs. Once we understand what's driving others' behavior, we're capable of either helping them with a change that might be helpful to them or having much better empathy for the reasons they behave as they do. At the very least, we'll keep in touch with what we truly have control over, and we'll understand other people and be able to predict their behavior.

Learn from Others

Sometimes we can learn valuable lessons from others who we realize are operating under beliefs that empower them.

I'm always interested in discovering the differences between successful distributors and those who are not as successful. One difference that I have noticed is that successful distributors invariably share the opportunity with everyone, especially those of a higher socioeconomic status. Conversely, less successful distributors seem to focus on recruiting only those people who are at their own level or lower. As I have considered this phenomenon, I've come to the conclusion that this is yet another example of operating under either empowering or hindering beliefs.

Sharing the opportunity with those of a socioeconomic level that is either equal to or less than your own relies on the belief that what you have to offer isn't worth the time or attention of those who might be living at a different level. Perhaps you might be saying, "Because Joe is already successful and doing so well, he would never be interested in signing up to be a distributor." This devaluation of the opportunity not only keeps you from sharing it, but it also adversely affects your self-esteem need. After all, if the opportunity is good enough for you, but not good enough for someone you respect, what does that say about who you are?

Switching gears, sharing the opportunity with those of a higher socioeconomic status reveals a different belief on your Belief Lens. What I have seen of successful distributors has shown me that they truly believe that they have an opportunity that can, will, and does change lives for the better—and it's a blessing that everyone needs in their lives. When you operate under the belief that "This opportunity can help everyone to better their lives," you'll never be hesitant or afraid of approaching everyone you know, regardless of socioeconomic status. That confidence has a positive effect on how you approach people, which increases the likelihood of them accepting the invitation to learn more.

If the "This opportunity can help everyone to better their lives" belief doesn't work for you, then perhaps another belief will. For instance, what about the belief that approaching people of a higher socioeconomic status about the opportunity will open a new market of potential recruits, thus increasing your chances of success? Believing that talking to everyone opens up new doors that will lead to your eventual success can be an empowering belief that can push you to achieve your personal best.

I have seen similar situations where distributors who seem content with the size of their organizations don't continue building. But after going through the "Why Drill," they discover that the belief on their lens is something like, "I'm not recruiting new people because I'm afraid they'll reject me." Because they fear rejection, they miss out on the chance to share a great opportunity with truly fantastic people that could propel their businesses to the next level. Using the "Why Drill" in such situations would be of great value in helping to identify hindering beliefs that hold us back from where we want to be.

Instant Replay

Key Points

- We can identify hindering beliefs by applying the "Why Drill."

- Once hindering beliefs are identified, they should be substituted with theoretically empowering beliefs.

- Our needs will not be met over time if they are based on external things.

Personal Exercise

- Look at different areas of your life (family, job, health) and identify your behavior patterns (habits) in each.

- Apply the "Why Drill" to identify what beliefs are driving those behavior patterns.

- Visualize new, better behavior patterns in those areas (how would you like your life to be?).

- Identify theoretical beliefs that would drive those new behavior patterns.

Where Do We Go from Here?

In chapter twelve, we'll begin to look at specific ways we can implement new beliefs in our lives that will promote real growth.

CHAPTER TWELVE

PRACTICE MAKES PERCEPTION

Creating experiences, both actual and visualized, is the secret behind imprinting new beliefs. You can't believe what you haven't experienced.

S am Snead, the legendary golfer, had a favorite expression he used when he played in Pro-Ams. "The trouble with most amateurs," he would observe, "is they never hit the ball with their practice swing."

His point was wry, but apt. He'd watch a smooth, controlled practice swing as his amateur partner would warm up for the real thing. Then the real thing would come and it would bear little or no resemblance to the practice swing. It would be at least twice as fast and twice as hard. And, unfortunately, it would yield roughly the same result as the thousands of too fast, too hard "real" swings that had preceded it.

In golf as well as most everything else, we are creatures of habit. We can want to do things differently. We can plot and plan and scheme to depart from the way we've performed in the past. Using golf as a case in point, we can pay for thousands of dollars of lessons, subscribe to all the top instructional magazines, spend hundreds of hours beating balls on the driving range, and buy all the latest clubs. We can learn what we're supposed to do, and we can really want to do it.

Then we come to the difficult part. We go to the first tee and play for real and the hardest thing of all—a lot harder than paying for all those lessons—is to really change our swing.

Habits Aren't Easy to Change

Think about the way you live your life. Think about the habits you've reinforced over time, year in and year out. Those habits, good or bad, empowering or hindering, make up who you are and what you do. We are our habits, whatever they may be.

When I raced competitively, I had my own way of running the steeplechase, my own game plan. It was unique to me. I would always start at the back of the pack, very often in last place. I did this for what I came to realize were two good reasons: One, by staying out of the pack I avoided all the early jostling and pushing that typically went on as the race proceeded past the various obstacles, hurdles, and water jumps. Two, over time I came to the realization that I had a decent kick that, if conserved properly, could carry me past the field on the final lap. If my pace was right, I knew I could count on enough sprint speed to make up the ground.

As you might guess, this tactic tended to produce more than a little anxiety for friends, family, and supporters watching from the stands. If you didn't know my strategy—and even if you did—it was hard to watch. For most of the race, I'd be well in back of the pacesetters, right on the edge, it would seem, of disaster. Then, usually with about a lap or a lap and a half to go, I'd start moving my way up, and the question was always whether I could make up that much ground that quickly. At the very least, it was never boring.

So that was my habit, and over time it became automatic. I almost couldn't burst to the front of a race even if I tried.

For me that strategy worked well enough. I was able to compete on an international level for thirteen years, so it was understandable why I stuck with it. I can look back and accurately call it an "empowering" habit for me. I still reflect with amusement on the few times I tried to deviate from that strategy—as an experiment or because I was in a field where I thought I might be better off just taking off—and how I couldn't do it very easily. Even on those occasions when I wasn't racing a strategic steeplechase and was going only for a specific time, I had a difficult time turning off that old impulse of assuming what became known as "my customary position in the rear."

There is a Natural Law that explains why habits are so hard to break. It states:

Whenever the mind is presented with opposing beliefs, it will naturally seek to reduce the conflict.

If there's a conflict, the mind will naturally first seek to reduce the conflict by going to the most familiar and comfortable route. And, that's going to be the one we're used to.

Do you remember back in chapter two when we first discussed the imprinting process? Well, over time these imprints create superhighways of synapses as we constantly commute over them and reaffirm their route.

So it is that when we stand over a golf ball and we're absolutely determined to use a new swing, when it comes down to crunch time, we'll still, to our astonishment, use the old swing.

We Can Change

When Sam Snead said, "The trouble with most amateurs is they never hit the ball with their practice swing," note that he said most. He didn't mean all amateurs, and he couldn't mean that was a condition for life. The only reason that statement has so much universal truth is because it is typically correct. The typical amateur usually plays golf about once a week, if he or she is lucky, and consequently that doesn't offer nearly enough time and energy to create new imprints that will facilitate a smooth transition from the old bad swing to a new good swing—to a "real" swing that is like the practice swing.

Practice makes perception, in other words. Left alone, our imprints will perpetuate themselves our whole lives, leaving us more and more powerless to change as time goes on. Unless we first create a conflict by introducing new theoretical beliefs onto our Belief Lens, and then set to work making that new opposing belief stick, we'll always be a slave to the same old imprints as stamped by the same old beliefs. So the question, and the challenge, becomes: How do we turn the new theoretical belief into reality so that it will drive behavior that will meet our needs over time?

Can't Eat Just One

To answer that, let's use an example I think we might all be able to relate to. Let's say our current behavior is to go home after work, when we're tired and hungry, and the first thing we do when we walk in the door is grab a big bag of potato chips from the pantry and start munching away. Since we can't eat just one, before we know it we're to the bottom of the bag. Then we recline on the couch, click on the TV, and either watch television or take a nap, or both.

In this experience, what are the positive consequences of our actions? Well, we're not hungry anymore, we're relaxed, and we're getting some rest that feels good. What are the negative consequences? Well, we haven't done much for our body fat, we've raised our cholesterol count, and we won't feel much like moving when we decide it's time to get off the couch. We're sluggish and tired, and later on, when we should go to bed, we're not going to be tired.

Notice that the positive consequences are all immediate and the negative consequences are the ones that don't manifest until later on.

Aware of these negative consequences as we sit there on the couch, feeling full but now somewhat disappointed in ourselves, we say, "I'm not going to do this any more. From now on I'm going to eat only healthy, balanced meals. I'm going to go to the grocery store after work and I'm going to buy some healthy food. I'll be healthier, I'll have more energy, and I'll reduce my weight." That's our new theoretical belief. It's not yet reality. Notice that it's based on positive consequences that will not be immediate and negative consequences (or what we see as negative consequences) that are more immediate, such as needing to make that trip to the store after work, the new need to cook, and the need to delay our hunger until all that is accomplished. Plus, we've got to give up the potato chips.

That's what we're confronted with the next day after work. We're tired and hungry again, and we've got two choices. We can go home, grab the chips, eat the whole bag, turn on the TV, and doze, or we can apply our new belief and go to the store, buy healthy food, take it home, cook it, and eat it.

What are we likeliest to do? Go home and eat the chips and flop on the couch, of course. Why? Because even though we've produced a conflict, we'll still naturally gravitate toward solving that conflict with the easiest and most immediate solution, which is doing what we've always done. It's human nature to seek the immediate solution; take care of the now right now. Human nature takes us to the biggest path, the most familiar path, the strongest synapse superhighway. We'll go to the strong imprint, the one with the least resistance, the familiar one.

Our Tendency Is to Take the Easy Way Out

It's the same with exercise or any of a thousand other examples we could name. We'll say, "OK, I've got a new belief that says exercise is good and I'm going to exercise daily." Then we'll go home and we'll think, "But I sure love reading the paper, and I don't want to miss the news on TV." Which of the conflicting behaviors will bring us immediate gratification, and which will bring us long-term benefit? Human nature will throw us to immediate gratification every time, and our tendency will always be to take that route. Human nature will have us reading the paper and watching the news—the things we've always done and the things that bring us immediate pleasure. The things that take care of our short-term needs are naturally going to be the most attractive in the short term.

This does not mean, of course, that we are powerless to shuck off the old and get on with the new. It just means that it's not easy, and we shouldn't be surprised when it isn't. Only through dedicated practice and determination can we go from the theoretical to reality by truly creating imprints that result in bigger habits than those we're trying to replace.

That practice and dedication is incumbent upon two other Natural Laws, the first of which says:

A belief is not written on my Belief Lens until it is reflected in my behavior.

Behavior does not lie. Behavior is always an accurate reflection of a belief on a Belief Lens. You can say to yourself or to others, "I believe junk food is bad for me." That's the belief you say is on your Belief Lens. But then you eat a donut. Why are you eating a donut? It might be because you're "going to run it off tonight" or because "it's only one donut." There's a belief you have on your Belief Lens that says eating a donut is acceptable, which in turn says your statement, "I believe junk food is bad for me," is not entirely an adopted belief. No matter how much you insist it is, it can't be. Why? Because you're eating that donut, that's why. That's your behavior, and behavior does not lie.

This is true, too, for groups, organizations, and businesses. I have had a chance to observe many different environments, many varied work atmospheres, and it's not at all difficult to make pretty accurate guesses as to what beliefs are on a company's Belief Lens. As an example, I once did some work with the Caterpillar company in Chicago, and as I drove into their plant the first thing I noticed was a big sign that said QUALITY PEOPLE WORKING TOGETHER TO MAKE QUALITY PRODUCTS. Inside the plant I saw the same sign everywhere I turned. There were all kinds of variations on the "Quality" theme, all of them presenting the same basic company belief of quality products being produced by quality people. The interesting thing I saw in the Caterpillar employees as I worked with them was that they believed that company value. I could see it by their behavior. They acted like quality people. They walked, talked, and worked like quality people. The imprinting, it appeared to me, had taken hold. Their quality behavior reflected that. They truly saw themselves as quality people working together to make quality products.

We Need Structure

Realizing that our behavior conforms to our beliefs, whether we're consciously aware of it or not, only further emphasizes the importance of operating with beliefs that empower us. If our behavior reflects hindering beliefs, we need to go about changing our beliefs.

That brings us to the second Natural Law, which says:

> *Structuring new experiences is the most effective*
> *way to create and reinforce new beliefs.*

There are three kinds of structured experiences—Actual, Visualized, and Modeling—which are necessary to complete the process of cementing new beliefs onto our Belief Lens.

Let's examine these structured experiences by using the example of giving a speech. First, let's imagine that we want to create a belief on our

Belief Lens that says, "I am good at giving speeches." We know that only with that belief in place can we then drive behavior that will produce good speech-making qualities. Since we have no real history of giving good speeches, this new belief of ours is going to need some help in getting established.

This is where the structuring comes in.

Our initial impulse, of course, would probably be to give a speech. That would qualify, of course, as an Actual Experience. To do this, we would seek out an opportunity to give a speech; we would conquer any fears we have such as shyness or pronunciation of words so we could physically walk to the podium, and then we would deliver our speech.

By carefully structuring that Actual Experience, we would begin the internal imprinting process that, we'd hope, over time would turn us into good speech-givers.

Let's say giving speeches isn't something we naturally feel comfortable about doing. Let's say it downright scares us to even think about getting up in front of an audience and giving a speech. We might not even make it to the microphone before we collapse. How can we ever possibly get to the point that we could not only give a speech, but give a good speech?

Visualizing Precedes the Deed

The answer is that Actual Experiences are often best preceded by Visualized Experiences.

In the case of the speech, visualizing would entail first seeing the audience in our minds, hearing the audience's applause, hearing the audience's laughter, and hearing ourselves use clear enunciation combined with a confident, powerful delivery. We'd do all this in our minds. We'd imagine conquering all our fears and concerns.

Visual structuring works because it's just as real to the mind as actual structuring. What we live in our mind, we record in our mind. That's what imprinting is. The moment we experience an event vividly in our imagination, it is recorded or imprinted as an experience, even though we didn't physically do it.

I personally never ran a race without first living it many times in my mind before I actually competed. I visualized warming up, how fast I was going to run, who else was going to be in the race, and what they would do. I visualized what I would do in case this circumstance or that circumstance came up. I visualized where I wanted to be at the end of each lap. I visualized how I would go over each hurdle. Three of the four times I set American records during my career, I had told my roommate that day in the hotel the lap times I planned to run that night for the record, and on all three occasions, I hit those lap times right on. Why? Because I'd already lived it. I'd experienced it. I was already programmed. (The other occasion I set a record was in the 1980 Olympic Trials and my visualizing was more on making the Olympic team than breaking the record). That's what happens when we visualize. We program our lives. We lay down the imprints that drive us.

As I said at the beginning of this chapter, on those occasions when I did run races for record times, I had to deviate from my usual strategy of running at the back of the pack. If I hadn't visualized extensively before getting to the starting line, I never would have been able to break that old habit of "laying back" long enough to do something different, if only for one night.

We're the Authors

The exciting part of the visualizing process—and this goes for the entire process of achieving our personal best through principle-driven behavior—is that we are the exclusive authors of it. We can make sure that it's enjoyable, rewarding, fulfilling, and satisfying. No matter what we want to accomplish, visualizing gives us the steering wheel to our lives. If we're first successful in our minds, we can then put ourselves in position to be successful in our actions.

Let's take a real "far out" example. Let's say we want to overcome a fear we have of skydiving. We're probably not going to go out and skydive a hundred times to conquer that fear. That might not be too advisable. Instead, what we can do is first practice skydiving vividly in our minds over and over, in preparation for that first jump. First we'll learn more about skydiving and all its intricacies. We'll watch videos of people skydiving safely, read books about overcoming fear, talk to people who have actually skydived and survived—and enjoyed it! Then, in our minds, in a relaxed moment, we'll imagine we're up in the plane preparing to jump. We'll feel the heaviness of the pack on our back, the awkwardness of the suit and the straps all around our body. We'll hear the engine of the plane roaring in our ears and the voices of the other jumpers as they shout to be heard above the noise.

We'll see the faces of our cojumpers, and they'll be excited, happy faces, looking forward to what they're about to experience. We're NOT going to imagine faces full of fear and anguish (least of all our own). Now we'll hear and smell and feel the rush of air as the door opens and the instructor says, "Step out onto the bar and hang on until I say to let go." Now we'll see ourselves stepping out and looking down! The wind is strong! The instructor says, "Hang on, hang on... NOW! Let go!" And we let go. We feel the air rushing by our ears. Now we find the ripcord and we PULL! Whoosh! All of a sudden, we're going up, up as the parachute opens. This is fun! Now we're floating, sailing through the air safely with the comfort of the parachute above us. We're floating. We're flying. We smell the air. We see the incredible, unobstructed 360-degree view that unfolds everywhere in front of our eyes. We feel the straps on our shoulders, our lifeline, and we feel that the straps are secure. We're floating, floating, floating. We're having an incredible experience! Now the ground is approaching rapidly and we're preparing to land. We're going over in our mind how to hit the ground so we won't hurt ourselves. We're going to land perfectly. Now the ground is rushing toward us. It's there. We bend and fold just right. Our knees absorb the shock. We do the roll perfectly as we glide to a stop. The parachute falls gracefully behind us. We stand up and feel exhilarated as we look back up at the sky!

Experiencing a parachute jump like that in our mind prepares us for the actual thing. It makes us want to skydive. Such visualizing can be effective in all areas of our lives. We can visualize talking assertively to our supervisor about a project we feel passionately about. We can visualize making an effective sales presentation. We can visualize taking a test for our pilot's license. We can visualize fly-fishing on the Madison River in Montana. We can visualize acting in a play. The list goes on and on. Visualizing is limited only by our imagination.

When visualizing helps us realize the establishment of a new belief it becomes an important step along the path of achieving our personal best through principle-driven behavior.

A Terrific Example

One of the best examples of visualizing—and resultant positive consequences—I've ever heard is the Viktor Frankl story as told in his book *Man's Search for Meaning*. Mr. Frankl was a prisoner in a concentration camp in Germany during World War II, and he tells a horrifying tale of suffering through conditions that were most inhumane. He was stripped of virtually everything physical. He was tortured, starved, and drugged, and made to live in conditions that tested human endurance. In virtually every physical sense, he was a prisoner. Yet he survived. His secret was in recognizing what he had control over and taking advantage of that. He didn't have control over much, but he did have control over his own thoughts. He had control over how he chose to respond to the horrible things done to him. He had control over where he went in his mind. He could see whatever he wanted—in his mind. He could visit wherever he wanted—in his mind. Through effective visualizing, Viktor Frankl survived, and in some ways, actually thrived.

Actual Experiences

Of course visualizing is only the first step, albeit an extremely important first step. Visualizing has to become a partner with Actual Experiences. Otherwise we'll spend our lives in a fantasy world. By visualizing ourselves behaving in a certain manner, we facilitate actually being that way, and every time we behave a certain way we strengthen an imprint, or belief, driving that behavior. So to make a new theoretical belief reality we must structure both Visualized and Actual Experiences in our lives to build new imprints until they are strong enough to overtake the old hindering beliefs.

As we have discussed, some of our old hindering beliefs will take a long time to be totally overcome because we have been "validating"— and hence strengthening—these hindering beliefs for many years. Other beliefs we can overcome in a matter of days or weeks. It's all going to take effort, but just how much effort can vary greatly.

For example, it took me a year and a half to have my new belief become operative when I switched careers. I didn't change my old belief to my new belief over night. Remember, my old belief was that my self-worth was dependent on how others viewed my profession and that being a lawyer caused others to view me as important. At first, I wasn't so sure about my new profession.

My new theoretical belief was that my self-worth was dependent on how I viewed my profession, and I needed to be in a profession that brought me fulfillment. Only by continually structuring new experiences consistent with my new belief was I able to gradually build the new imprints that over time replaced the old ones and validated the new theoretical belief I had put into place.

First I visualized myself enjoying my work and feeling fulfilled. Then I found a profession compatible with that vision. Then I tried Actual Experiences, actually working in that profession, to see if it would bring about the desired results. For me, it worked, as evidenced by my new behaviors, such as no more hump days or T.G.I.F.'s. Again, this was no overnight process. It took time to overcome the old belief. Only through these structured experiences was the process able to get to a physical change of jobs. Only after Actual Experiences was I able to change my response from, "I'm an attorney, I work at Franklin," to "I work at Franklin." Only after a good deal of work and effort at structuring new experiences was I able to realize that my new belief was in fact one that would better meet my needs.

Modeling

There's a third technique to help identify and reinforce our new beliefs. It is called Modeling. Modeling is identifying someone who has already implemented the behaviors in his life that we want in any given area of our lives. We then carefully study what our model is doing and has done to be successful and apply the same techniques in our lives.

The Community Commerce business uses modeling extensively. Successful distributors teach new distributors to "duplicate" what they have done. Wise new distributors "replicate" what successful distributors have done. They watch successful distributors closely, mimicking what they do to provide service to their customers, what they say to prospects to interest them in signing up, how they train their downline, and how they build their organizations. This experience of modeling successful distributors imprints a picture of success. Then, from this picture, new distributors can identify the experiences (tasks) they need to reinforce that imprint.

In other words, we don't have to reinvent the wheel. We can take advantage of someone else's years of experience as a starting point rather than our ending point. We can avoid their mistakes by watching them, consulting with them, or even reading about them. We are thus visualizing our path of success. All that is left for us to do is to implement those behaviors in our lives.

Instant Replay

Key Points

• Changing behavior isn't easy. We need to have a good game plan in place to really change.

• When the mind is presented with opposing beliefs, it will naturally seek to reduce the conflict and try to remain with the most reinforced beliefs.

• By structuring experiences—Actual, Visualized, and Modeling— we can override our mind's desire to maintain the status quo.

• Beliefs aren't truly written on our Belief Lens until they're reflected in our behavior.

Personal Exercise

• Identify the new beliefs you want to guide specific areas of your life. (See Personal Exercise, chapter eleven.)

• Structure experiences that will reinforce the new belief by doing the following:

1. Make a list of actual experiences (tasks) you can do starting today. (Focus on what can be done during the next three weeks.)

2. Visualize what success looks like in your focus area. (Mentally review that picture every day.)

3. Model your life after someone whose behavior reflects your picture of success.

4. Select a buddy to whom you can commit to acting on your plan. (If possible, select someone pursuing similar goals.)

• Write your structured experiences on task lists in your Day Planner. (Then act on them daily.)

Where Do We Go from Here?

In chapter thirteen, I'd like to continue the story I began in chapter three. What happened to me in the Olympic Games of 1984 and, most importantly, how I reacted to what happened, illustrates the importance of applying those two words "over time" to our beliefs.

CHAPTER THIRTEEN

PERSONAL PEACE

If I hadn't changed my beliefs, what happened in the Los Angeles Olympic Games would still haunt me today.

The hardest part was the waiting. It was a warm, almost muggy, Los Angeles twilight as I stretched my leg muscles on the warm-up track adjacent to the Los Angeles Memorial Coliseum. In an hour I would compete in the steeplechase final of the 1984 Los Angeles Olympic Games. It was an event I had been waiting for most of the past decade, ever since I decided not to quit the track team at BYU in January of 1976, fueled by my new beliefs.

I was thirty years old, and this wasn't my first Olympic experience. My first Olympic Games had been in Montreal in 1976, where I roomed with Bruce Jenner, who set a world record in the decathlon—thanks in no small part, I will forever believe, to my Jethro Tull collection of eight-track tapes, which Jenner listened to faithfully each night in preparation for the next day's competition.

I finished tenth in the Montreal Olympics and was the top placing American in my race. All in all, a heady experience for a guy no one had heard anything about; a guy who needed to wear a "Hello, my name is…" tag wherever he went. My time of 8:23.9 in the Montreal final meant I had lowered my personal best time by just over one minute in less than seven months—and was within seven-tenths of a second of the fastest steeplechase ever run by an American. If anybody needed more encouragement to keep running, if anybody needed extra motivation to see what was over the next hill, well, it wasn't me.

I was well aware of where I stood in the international scheme of things, and that there were some intriguing possibilities on the horizon, but I was determined to keep that competitiveness in check. I wanted to be sure I continued to subscribe to my new belief of concentrating on my own effort and not on the effort of others. To that end, I continued to be something of a loner on the workout track, a maverick who kept his head down, his eyes only on his own stopwatch. I had seen what happened when I looked at others and not at myself.

Thanks, in part, to excellent coaching along the way—first from James Blackwood and Al Rowan, my high school track coaches, to Sherald James at BYU, and then from Bill Bowerman, the head coach at the University of Oregon and a pioneer at Nike, who took me under his wing—and blessed, too, with reasonably good health, I thrived on the international circuit. The post-Montreal days were good ones for me. I set a new American record; won national championships in 1978, 1979, and 1980; and won several world-class races, including the Pan American Games in 1979 and the big pre-Olympic meet in Russia called Spartakaide. By the time I made my second United States Olympic Team in 1980, I was ranked number four in the world and my winning time in the United States Olympic Trials was the fastest that year anywhere in the world.

At that point, my Olympic hopes, along with every other member of the U.S. team, were blindsided by political unrest. Because those 1980 games were to be held in Moscow, the capital of the Soviet Union, and because the Soviets invaded Afghanistan in January of 1980, our president, Jimmy Carter, elected to protest that invasion by pulling the U.S. team out of the Moscow Games.

It was a tough pill to swallow, I'll be the first to admit. In the world of track and field, the Olympics are the litmus test of your career, and each career doesn't get many such litmus tests. I was twenty-six years old in 1980 and dreamed of wearing an Olympic medal around my neck, perhaps even a gold medal, and it was no small disappointment to get over the dashing of that chance, especially since I could see no correlation between world politics and me running a steeplechase race in a sports gathering dedicated to peace and the brotherhood of man.

Still, as Moscow came and went, I ran on. I managed to graduate from law school at the University of Oregon and began my practice as an attorney. But it was running that remained my passion, and the Olympic Games of 1984 became my new ideal, my lighthouse on the shore. Surely we wouldn't boycott an Olympics we would host. To that end, I successfully won four more consecutive national titles and lowered the American record again. In 1981 and 1982, I was the number one ranked steeplechaser in the world, and in 1983 I was ranked number two. In Los Angeles, competing on my home turf, so to speak, I would be the favorite even if I didn't want to be.

That favored status was only increased when the Soviet Bloc countries announced they would not be coming to Los Angeles. The way they saw it, one boycott deserved another. That meant a number of good steeplechasers, including Boguslaw Maminski of Poland, ranked number three in the world, would not be in the field.

When Patriz Ilg of West Germany, the man who was ranked number one in the world in 1983, pulled out of the Olympics because of tonsillitis, the way to the gold medal was as prepared for Henry Marsh as it could be. I couldn't argue with that. A lot of excellent runners would still be competing, of course, but there was no question that I would be the favorite. I knew it and so did everyone else who had a passing knowledge of my event.

To that end, I became something of a celebrity, or at least as much of a celebrity as a person can become who participates in an event he first has to explain. The American TV networks all did profiles on who I was, where I'd come from, that kind of thing. Camera crews would fly into Salt Lake City and drive to our home in Bountiful, an adjoining suburb, where I would trace my history the best I could and try to be colorful. I cut back on my workload at the law firm to about 50 percent so I could fit in all the distractions and still leave room for quality workouts. The last thing I wanted to do was neglect my training. Every few weeks during the early part of 1984, I would fly to Los Angeles and meet Coach Bowerman, who would put me through simulated racing conditions in the Olympic climate. If we could help it, the L.A. smog was not going to be foreign to me or my lungs.

I should add that I thoroughly enjoyed all of it. I enjoyed running the steeplechase, and I enjoyed the atmosphere of the Olympic Games. I enjoyed the opportunities that were presented, I enjoyed being number one, and I enjoyed getting the chance to be a part of the Olympic Games again. I enjoyed the contract I signed with Nike. I enjoyed the endorsement deals that were lining up. These were dreams come true, goals accomplished, and I can honestly say I was thrilled with the process.

But I wasn't thrilled when I got sick.

The doctors told me it was a virus. They didn't know for sure which virus, but they knew for certain that not only was it a virus, it was a powerful virus.

If I could have personally chosen the worst possible time to hear this news, it would have been precisely when I heard it. It was in late June of

1984, just a few days after the U.S. Track and Field Olympic Trials had been held at the Los Angeles Coliseum, soon to be the site of the Olympic Games. The Trials, which constituted the 1984 U.S. championships, had gone as well as I'd hoped. I ran last most of the race and then used a healthy kick to win comfortably. It was my seventh straight national championship, and that pleased me; it extended a string of unbeaten races that stretched back almost a full year. It looked like everything was coming together. If I were a betting man, I'd have bet on myself. For the past six months, I had paid close attention to my diet and tried to rest as much as possible, and, as I said, I cut down on my legal practice—all in concert with my Olympic game plan.

Maybe I inadvertently overworked getting ready for the U.S. Trials, or maybe I was just unlucky. I don't know. But I do know that a week after the Trials and five weeks before the start of the Olympic Games in Los Angeles, I was flat in bed, felled by a bug of mysterious origin.

I rested and then tried to rest some more. Talk about your conflicts! I had a classic dilemma on my hands. On the one hand, I knew the very best way to beat a virus was to rest. On the other hand, I knew the very best way to lose an Olympic medal was to rest.

I tried to compromise.

I'd take just so much of my bed, and then I'd get up and work out. I couldn't help myself. Above all, a runner has to run. I remember one day at home in Bountiful when I got out of bed after a full day of taking it easy and then got on the treadmill and ran ten miles at my normal six minute-per-mile training pace.

After that I reached for my training log, quickly scribbled, "Not feeling 100 percent," and collapsed back into bed. I was a pathetic sight.

I couldn't shake this thing, whatever it was, and instinctively I knew it. It had its own course to run, that virus, and it was running it.

I went to Eugene, Oregon, for a pre-Olympic race but shouldn't have. I lost for the first time in nearly a year and for the first time ever to my

American teammate, Brian Diemer, who was trying to work up a good dose of confidence heading into the L.A. games. At least I was helping somebody's preparation.

I flew to Los Angeles for the first day of the Olympics, where I marched with the United States team in the spectacular opening ceremonies held in the coliseum. I enjoyed the spectacle as President Ronald Reagan opened the games of the Twenty-third Olympiad, and more than 90,000 spectators cheered the world's Olympians as they marched onto the track. By many accounts, those L.A. games turned out to be among the best ever staged, and no one could argue that they weren't launched in grand style. But as for me, I know I'd have enjoyed the festivities more if it hadn't been for the dizzy, lightheaded feeling.

Determined to rest and relax, I didn't stay in the Olympic Village with the rest of the athletes. I checked into the home of a family friend in Beverly Hills, where I reasoned that I could get plenty of down time with a minimum of distractions. I didn't think it would help my chances any if I spent my days in the Olympic Village. For one thing, I wouldn't get much rest amid all the commotion in the village. For another, the less my opponents knew about my condition, the better. I was determined to be a recluse.

It did help. Luckily, the steeplechase wasn't first on the Olympic program. I had more than a week after the opening ceremonies before my first qualifying heat was scheduled, another day before my second qualifying heat (providing I survived the first one), and a day between that heat and the final, to be held on the second-to-last day of the games.

The virus and the Olympic final were playing a game of chicken, and I was coming along for the ride.

I made it out of the first heat, placing fourth among the six finalists who moved on to the semifinals. In the semis I again weathered the crowd, again finishing fourth in a race that qualified six into the finals. Virus or no virus, I would be one of twelve runners who, in the early evening of August 10, 1984, would compete in the Olympic final, racing for the three medals at the finish line.

All of which brought me to the coliseum's warm-up track an hour before race time where, as I stretched, I tried to get a grip on everything I was feeling.

As I listened to the hum of 90,000 voices inside the stadium, and as I tried to coax a hamstring to go to new lengths, I gave myself a pregame talk. What I said to myself was that I was about to compete in a race that, for whatever reasons, would be very important to me. It was what I had set my sights on, what I had trained for, what I had designated as significant for most of my adult life—and since that was the case, when I got inside the stadium and they finally fired the gun that sent us off, I needed to make certain I didn't hold anything back.

I needed to give it all I had. That was my pep talk. Everything. Virus or no virus, alibi or no alibi, that's what I needed to do. If that got me the gold medal, fantastic! If it got me last place…well, that would be all right, too. The important thing was that after the race was over, I could look myself in the mirror and be able to say in the affirmative that I gave it my all.

That done, I walked into the coliseum. I had no idea what to expect. Probably the last thing I expected was to see Mary Decker-Slaney being carried off the track in the arms of her husband, Richard Slaney.

Mary Decker, as she had been known throughout her illustrious running career, was a close friend as well as an Olympic teammate. We ran for the same club, Athletics West, and our careers had connected in many ways. She was a multiple-time national champion and had won many major middle-distance races all around the world. In 1983, she won the world championship at 3,000 meters and was the favorite at that distance in Los Angeles as well. The only trophy not on her shelf was an Olympic medal—Mary, too, had been a casualty of the 1980 Moscow boycott—and L.A.'s home turf was seen as her place of redemption. In many ways, our stories paralleled each other. Both of us came to the games of 1984 with high hopes and high expectations—and a good deal of attention. Along with the sprinter and long jumper Carl Lewis, we were America's track-and-field odds-on favorites in 1984.

And now here was Mary, lying limply in the arms of her husband as he carried her to medical attendants who were waiting at the side of the track. Out on the track I noticed that the women's 3,000-meter race was still going on. I soon learned that there had been a collision just beyond the halfway point of the race. Mary and Zola Budd, a South African running for Great Britain, had collided, and Mary had crashed to the track, unable to continue the race. A shaken Budd ran on but, although she was leading at the time of the collision, faded to seventh place. Maricica Puica of Romania crossed the finish line first to claim the gold medal—not far from where Mary, in an obvious state of physical and mental anguish, was unsuccessfully trying to choke back the tears.

My heart went out to my friend and teammate. I knew how she felt and how painful that moment was for her. She did not deserve this. An already sober evening had just turned even more sober. With that in mind, I reported to the starting line for the beginning of the Olympic final in the men's 3,000-meter steeplechase. I hoped it wasn't an omen.

I was off with the gun, more or less. I assumed my customary position in the rear and let my head clear. It felt good to be running. It felt good to have the wait over. It felt good to finally be doing this. There were some good runners in the field but I was comforted by the fact that none had personal-best times as low as mine—a statistic by now well known to anyone listening to television or reading the newspapers. If I just had the stamina….

As the race wore on it became obvious to me, from my backseat position, that two Kenyans with the same first name, Julius Korir and Julius Kariuki, were going to have to be dealt with. Neither of the Juliuses had an international reputation—as was often the case with talented

Kenyans who tended to materialize at the Olympic Games—but I could tell by the way they were running that they had the talent to be in it for the long haul. The same went for Joseph Mahmoud, a proven commodity from France who was ranked fifth in the world, and, of course, for my teammate Diemer. I kept them all in sight.

With a lap to go I was right where I wanted to be and feeling OK so far. I was running on adrenaline, and so far, so good. I just hoped I wouldn't be too weakened for the stretch run, when my reserve of stamina would really be needed.

I moved from seventh to fifth. Then, on the back straightaway I passed, in order, Mahmoud, Diemer, and Kariuki. I was at the shoulder of the second Kenyan, Korir, as Al Michaels, the ABC commentator broadcasting the race, said, "And here comes Marsh!" Three hundred yards, one water jump, and one final barrier stood between this moment and the Olympic gold medal.

Much as I wanted to make Michaels look good, I never did get past Korir. I came to his shoulder, maybe six inches from taking the lead, but he held me off and stayed in front; by the water jump at the last corner he had extended his lead to several yards. He went over the water first, then me. Mahmoud and Diemer soon followed, with Kariuki fading.

Less than one hundred meters to go, it became obvious that Korir was going to be one tough Kenyan to catch. Meanwhile, there's the Frenchman and my American teammate to worry about. At the final barrier Mahmoud surged past me. He wasn't going to be easy to catch either. Up ahead, Korir was breaking the tape for the win and the gold medal, and Mahmoud was closing fast to take the silver. The bronze medal would go to one of two Americans—me or the one closing quickly behind me.

My teammate passed me just before we crossed the line. Brian Diemer beat me out for the bronze medal by nineteen-hundredths of a second. Less than two feet.

Fourth place was mine. As I said then and still say, "Fourth place, the worst possible finish. You don't get a medal, and you still have to go through drug-testing."

Only for me the drug-testing had to wait. As soon as I crossed the thin white line that said "you can stop now," I collapsed onto the track and fell quite unconscious. I have watched the videotape of that race many times since and still find it curious to view myself going through something I have no memory of. As the other runners finished, several stooped down to see if I was all right, looking curiously at this crumpled figure who only moments before had been ahead of them on the back straightaway, going for broke.

Within moments an ambulance drove onto the track and a team of paramedics lifted me onto a stretcher and into the back of the ambulance, which transported me to the small infirmary that adjoins the coliseum. The crowd didn't know what was wrong with me and, at that moment, neither did I.

As it turned out, nothing was wrong except I had run out of fuel, gas, combustion, whatever you want to call it. My body had taken over and simply shut down. It wasn't going an inch farther. It was as simple as that. About thirty minutes later I regained consciousness in the infirmary and swung my feet off the cot and onto the floor. I walked to the parking lot and drove myself home.

The next day, and for several days after that, the commotion hit. To this day I'm amazed at the compassion and outpouring of empathy that took place. I got telegrams and cards and letters from all around the country, commiserating with my bad turn of luck. At the track the next night, I was personally inundated by well-meaning supporters who shook their heads and said, "too bad," and "that must be devastating."

Now don't get me wrong. I appreciated then, and still do, the genuine affection and empathy that was displayed. Many people showed kindness. Perfect strangers expressed their sympathy. But no sooner was the 1984

Olympic final over than I honestly felt none of the devastation and gut-wrenching defeat many people expected I would—and that many of them were feeling.

I was disappointed, to be sure. I don't think I'll ever forget the frustration I felt that August night in the summer of 1984. I didn't stop being human. I wanted that gold medal as much as anyone (I also wouldn't have minded the $40,000 bonus Nike, one of my sponsors, was offering if I won it).

But I wasn't kidding when I said I could live with what happened. I wasn't kidding when I said it was disappointing, to be sure, but it was hardly devastating. In my own mind, it was just the opposite. As far as I was concerned, I had won. The reason was because I had satisfied my own game plan, my own belief. Winning the gold medal wasn't my game plan. Giving it all I had was my game plan. I did that. I could not argue with myself that I had given it everything I had when I collapsed unconscious just beyond the finish line.

The same belief that enabled me to rejoin my college track team after I quit some eight years before was anchored even more securely on my Belief Lens by the time the Olympic Games of 1984 came along. For me, that turned out to be a good thing. A very good thing.

Just why I was lucky enough to stumble—and I did stumble—upon the concept of principle-driven behavior when I was twenty-one years old I'm not sure. But I count it as one of the most significant stumbles of my life. Without an empowering belief on my Belief Lens in Los Angeles, I could have been saddled with a devastation that would have been enormous. I have seen other athletes in similar situations, and I know it can be debilitating if you're not careful.

Certainly I have often reflected on the coincidence surrounding my experience in Los Angeles and the experience of my friend and teammate, Mary Decker-Slaney. Both of us had to deal with an Olympic experience that didn't conclude as we'd hoped for—a medal hanging from our necks as the national anthem was played and the Stars and Stripes raised up the flagpole. That was tough for a couple of veteran performers and prerace favorites. Mary's reaction was different from mine. Her grief was more profound, her outrage more pronounced, for what I think are very understandable reasons. I'm sure her Belief Lens reflected belief that said you were successful when you beat other people—just as mine once had. That being the case, when you don't beat other people, your necessities are going to be severely threatened, and that's difficult to deal with. Mary carried that Los Angeles "defeat" with her for a long time. It affected how she raced in the future. It affected her affection for running. All because of the beliefs on her Belief Lens. Both of us could say life hadn't been fair because of external obstacles—for me the virus and for her the runner who tripped her up—but how we dealt with that realization, how we chose to behave in response, depended on the beliefs that drove us. We were bound to them.

There was a remarkable moment in Atlanta during the 1996 Summer Olympics with Mary Decker-Slaney twelve years after her mishap with Zola Budd. Through years of injuries Mary kept at it. As in 1984, Mary did not make it to the medal stand; in fact, in 1996 she was eliminated in a preliminary round. However, her response to not winning a medal was very different. In 1996, she was satisfied with the opportunity to be able to compete in the Olympics at what was considered an "old age." Her belief and driving force was no longer centered on winning. It was now based on being able to compete and give it her best shot.

It's our beliefs that determine how we're going to behave in any situation; it's our beliefs that allow us to be in control of our lives or out of control. Our beliefs determine if life's whims are going to decide when and where we land, or if we'll decide that ourselves. Applying empowering beliefs and behaving accordingly is the key to a healthy, happy life. I am convinced of that. I still wish I had a gold medal hanging from my fireplace mantel. But I know I can live, and I know I can still feel self-worth, without it.

Instant Replay

Key Points

- Having an empowering belief in place allowed me to appreciate my Olympic experience even without a gold medal—or any medal for that matter—draped around my neck.

- Our success is measured by personal beliefs, not by anybody else's standards or beliefs.

Personal Exercise

- Identify examples in your life where you had an "empowering belief" which was different from others around you (boss, spouse, coworker, child, neighbor, upline, downline, customer).

- Identify examples in your life where you judged other people by your beliefs when your beliefs were not empowering for those people.

Where Do We Go from Here?

In chapter fourteen, we'll go through a step-by-step process for employing new personal beliefs.

CHAPTER FOURTEEN

PRACTICAL APPLICATION

So you really want to change a belief? Here's how.

By now we've established this core truth: The quality of our lives is going to be no better, and no worse, than the strength of our beliefs.

Empowering beliefs will drive behavior that will produce results that will satisfy our needs over time.

Hindering beliefs will drive behavior that will produce results that will not satisfy our needs over time.

End of discussion.

When we accept this core truth, our search for happiness, peace, and fulfillment will focus only on beliefs, our own beliefs. No matter how much money we might have or how many cars, toys, or houses; no matter how often our picture is in the paper or how many times we've visited the White House; no matter where we went to college, where we live, who we know, or where we work, all of these are ineffective at meeting our needs over time if our beliefs hinder us.

Think about people you know, people you've studied, people you see on television, in the movies, or in sporting events. Look at their lives. Do some appear happy? Do some appear tormented? Does it seem to matter whether they're rich or poor, famous or anonymous, short or tall, white or brown?

The answer, of course, is no. It doesn't seem to matter. You can take two people with nearly identical circumstances, and one can be quite content with life and the other in constant conflict with it. What's the difference? What's the answer to this mystery?

Empowered Means Contented

The answer is beliefs. If you knew what their beliefs were, it wouldn't be a mystery at all. The contented person is driven by beliefs that are empowering for him or her. The person with conflict is driven by beliefs that are hindering him or her.

Whether we realize it consciously or not (and many times we do not), it's our empowering beliefs that are our most valuable possession. They're far more valuable than wealth, fame, youth, good looks, a good curve ball, or winning the lottery.

None of these assets—valuable though they might be—can do what empowering beliefs do. Empowering beliefs are what drive us to behave in a way that helps us to consistently meet our needs—all four of them— over time. Our needs to live, to love, to enjoy, and to have self-esteem are all satisfied when we have empowering beliefs in place. What could be more valuable than that? It's our empowering beliefs that can help us accept life on all its terms, both the fair and the unfair. It's our empowering beliefs that help us flow with the things we can't control, instead of fighting upstream against them. It's our empowering beliefs that help us understand those things we can control and use them to our advantage.

Affordable to All

The good news is that, despite the fact that you couldn't put a price on their value, creating empowering beliefs is something we can all do, regardless of our circumstances. We can all "afford" them. Empowering beliefs don't cost anything to acquire, at least not in terms of cash up front. They don't weigh anything. They're easy to carry. They do not discriminate. There's no age limit, no race limits, no favoritism, no quotas, and no politics involved. And the supply is unlimited. You can't have too many.

One thing empowering beliefs don't have is a written owner's manual. They don't come with one. They don't come with instructions on how to put them together, how to maintain them, and how to fix them. They're not clearly marked so we can identify the empowering beliefs from hindering beliefs.

In our effort to better facilitate change through empowering beliefs, there's nothing to stop us from putting together an owner's manual on our own.

Over the years, I've become a proponent of creating empowering beliefs before the pain makes us do it. We've discussed the billions of dollars and tens of millions of annual prescriptions to treat the "diseases of choice" that bring untold amounts of pain, suffering, low self-esteem, lost productivity, and lifelong regrets. We have control over the beliefs that drive these behaviors and responses. I've formulated a Five Step plan to help us better visualize and implement that control.

The Five-Step Plan

The Five Step plan is simply something tangible we can look at to help us better visualize reality. It can be very effective as an aid when you've come to the conclusion that beliefs are important and you'd like to have a systematic process to follow to implement the beliefs that will drive your peak performance.

These are the five steps:

1. Identify a stressor (person, situation, event, challenge) in your life and the associated habitual emotional responses to that stressor.

2. Identify the hindering belief and need(s) the stressor threatens by asking, "Why does the stressor make you respond with that emotion?" Follow that by asking, "So what? Why is that a threat to you?"

3. Identify your life's experiences that created and validated the hindering belief in the first place.

4. Identify a theoretical new empowering belief, or "Why Not," to replace the hindering belief.

5. Structure experiences (Actual, Visualized, and Modeling) to sufficiently imprint the new empowering belief so it becomes strong enough to replace the old hindering belief.

You'll find that the Five Step plan has universal applicability. It can be used in all facets of life: at home, at work, at play, within interpersonal relationships, anywhere and everywhere. Simply plug in the stressor of your choice in step one and proceed from there.

Remember, our definition of "stressor," as discussed in chapter five, is that it's an obstacle; it's something we see that gets in the way of us getting what we want. It's stressors that cause us unrest, anxiety, distress, pain—in a word, stress—as we respond to the perception of the threats. Stressors are what we perceive as obstacles getting in the way of where we'd like to go and achieving what we want. In turn, it's our response that creates the undesirable symptoms (discussed in chapter five).

Identify Stressors

Remember, too, that when we choose to deal with these symptoms or stressors we'll often turn to quick-fix remedies in an attempt to eliminate the discomfort we're feeling. These remedies range from over-the-counter drugs to prescription drugs, from oversleeping to obsessive shopping. It's a big list, and it can lead to big addictions—addictions that can keep us in the same stressful ruts indefinitely.

So it's important to first identify our stressor. Once we've successfully done that, we're ready to move on with the Five Step plan and the implementation of a new empowering belief on our personal Belief Lens.

For our purposes here, let's use a hypothetical workplace stressor and run it through the Five Step plan to see how it works. There are many stressors we could choose, but for the purposes of this example, let's use "No."

"No" is a common cause of stress in the Community Commerce industry—many distributors are afraid of hearing that simple, two-letter word. "No" causes a lot of people a lot of grief. From a practical standpoint, there's nothing that threatening about hearing "No." we hear that response to so many questions throughout the day that it usually just rolls right off our backs. But the prospect of hearing "No," keeps so many distributors from sharing the business opportunity with other people. Just the thought of a potential "No," freezes them in their tracks, keeping them from sharing and hindering their ability to build a successful business.

Yet, for some distributors, "No" isn't threatening or scary. They offer the chance to everyone, and when they encounter a "No," they shrug their shoulders and move on to the next person. Many distributors regard "No," as "Not right now," and don't let it knock them off of their stride. For these distributors, the belief on their Belief Lens is absolutely empowering. Just take a look at the size of their organizations.

For the purposes of our Five Step plan, we're going to say that "No" isn't inspiring for you at all. It's a bad word with an even nastier connotation. You perceive "No" as nothing less than a necessary evil that exists solely to haunt you and make your life miserable. For you, the prospect of hearing "No" to your invitation produces anxiety and irritability, increased blood pressure, a racing pulse—you have a strong desire to dive under the covers and go to sleep until it's all over.

You're afraid of "No." You're petrified of "No."

"No" is your stressor. Maybe you use drugs to deal with the pain it causes you, either over-the-counter drugs or perhaps something your doctor gives you. Maybe you have high blood pressure as the result of your fear of, "No," and you can feel an ulcer coming on. Maybe there are other addictions in your life that are the result of your aversion to "No"—addictions that circumvent the overall quality of your work and life and keep you from building a successful business.

Remember, this is just a hypothetical example. We're just imagining here. Hopefully, it's close enough to reality so you can relate to this exercise.

You've decided you've had enough pain associated with facing "No." You're tired of the anger, frustration, anxiety, and depression. You don't want to feel that way anymore. You don't want to take the drugs to try to deal with it. You don't want to feel like running away. You don't want the doctor to take your blood pressure and whistle. You want to find a new empowering belief that won't make you feel so helpless and out of control.

So, having identified your stressor and the habitual negative emotional responses that it drives, you go to step two. You want to identify the hindering belief and the need being threatened.

Begin by Asking Why

First you ask, "Why?"

"Why does 'No' cause frustration and anxiety?"

Let's say your first response as you engage in this self-talk is, "'No' makes me anxious because the person who said, 'No,' won't want to have a relationship with me anymore."

Then you ask, "So what? Why is it threatening to me if that person doesn't want to continue our relationship?" You answer, "Because we're friends, and I enjoy her company." (Hence the need being threatened is the need to enjoy, and the hindering belief is, "When a person says 'No,' she is not rejecting the opportunity, she's rejecting me.")

Notice every answer is a belief.

So we continue talking to ourselves.

"Why would the person be rejecting you?"

"Because if she says 'No,' then things will be awkward the next time we get together."

"Has she ever said 'No' to any other invitation that you've extended?"

"Well, yes."

"Were things awkward any other time that she turned down an invitation?"

"No."

"How would she feel about you sharing something that is important to you and that has blessed your life?"

"She'd probably appreciate that I care about her enough to share something like that."

"So why are you afraid of her saying 'No'?"

"Good question."

The Third Step: Third Grade

So you think deeper, and as you think deeper you move into step three of our Five Step plan. You examine your life experiences. You go back to the roots of where you got your beliefs. You go to your imprints. What do you find there? Well, for the sake of this example, let's say you go back to, of course, the ever-popular third grade.

It was in the third grade (or thereabouts) that you learned, for the first time, that "No" can mean more than just, "Thank you, but I'm not interested." Maybe an invitation was turned down so that the other person could play with someone else. Maybe you were made fun of. Maybe the person stopped being your friend.

Now you realize that you're afraid of "No" because you're still being driven by the belief you put on your Belief Lens way back then. You had a painful experience and it left an imprint that's turned into a superhighway by the time you're an adult.

As a consequence, you're still behaving as if you're in third grade. You got your belief in school. (Schools are no doubt the largest factory of imprints there is; where else do we have so many values and consequences imprinted on our minds?) Ever since, that belief has driven your behavior. It's still driving you all these years later, determining your response and your behavior today. As is often the case, through your penetrating "why?" questions, you've discovered that your perception is a lot worse than the reality.

Some of you may be saying, "But sometimes people do stop associating with me after I extend the invitation to learn more about the opportunity." Remember the Natural Law that says, "When my self-worth is dependent on something external, I will not meet my needs over time"? The same law applies for all of our needs. Whenever we base any need on something external—like the acceptance of others—it will drive negative behaviors and responses over time. Therefore we just learn to internalize our needs to find empowering beliefs.

Internal Is the Key

Now you're ready to implement step four. George Bernard Shaw said, "You see things as they are and ask, why? I dream things that never were and ask, why not?" That quote summarizes step four. Let's go back to our example. Now you want to identify a theoretical new belief or, "Why not," about "No" that bases meeting your need to enjoy on something over which you have control. It must be a belief that will drive behavior that will produce results that will satisfy your need to enjoy. You'll ask, "Can I base my need to enjoy on something over which I have control?" The answer is yes. You can control how you respond to a "No" even if you don't have control over whether the person will say "No" or not. You can do that by focusing on how you react to the "No" if it comes. Remember, your productivity will always go up when you focus on the things over which you have control.

In theory, then, you begin thinking about what new belief would eliminate your fear of "No" as a stressor. Why not, "When a person says 'No' to my invitation, they're not rejecting me. They may not be ready for the opportunity right now, or they may not be interested. But the things that first brought us together are still there. We can continue to be friends and enjoy each other's companionship."

Your theoretical new belief turns a "No" into a fleeting thing, just a part of one of many conversations that you've had with your friend. You're not going to look at "No" anymore worrying what will happen if someone tells you "No"; you're going to focus on building a relationship with the person and enjoying your time with him or her.

As we discussed in chapter three, note that the stressor, or obstacle, did not change. The only thing that changed was your perception of it. Armed with this new perception, your anxiety, your irritability, and all the rest of those negative responses—the essence of what we call stress—are eliminated.

But all this is still in theory for the moment. In step four all you've come up with is what you think the new belief ought to be. In step five, you will structure experiences that will make the new belief strong enough so it is capable of replacing the old one.

You Can Control Yourself

This is where the work comes in. This is where you have to meet head-on your body's predisposition to stay the same, to not rock the boat, to not change. Knowing your biggest opponent is, in fact, yourself gives you an edge—that is, if you'll take it. And what's the edge? The fact that you have control over yourself, that's what. Control is important. Control what you can, and can the rest. If we've built up addictions long enough or gotten especially good at masking the pain, we may think we can't control ourselves, and we may prove to be a formidable opponent for a time, but a beatable opponent nonetheless. If we're willing to put new beliefs on our Belief Lens, and give them a chance, we can eventually prevail.

In the case of your old (and powerful) hindering "No" belief vs. your new (and weak) empowering "No" belief, you decide to structure enough experiences so you will be able to slowly but surely turn the tables. First, you decide you want somehow to visualize the fun you'll have with a new friend or a strengthened relationship because they realized that you shared something incredibly important to you with them. Remember, they're not rejecting you when they say "No"—the perception in this case is much worse than the reality. You do all this in your mind, and it feels good!

After that, you decide you want to invite ten people every week for the next six months. You'll want to make sure that you're especially careful about how you react if someone does say "No." You want to make sure that you're friendly and open to their thoughts and opinions. Remember, your goal is to create a new belief about "No," one that drives behavior that produces results that meet your needs. You understand that to establish that belief, you're going to have to have patience, especially at the beginning. The imprint you're seeking will not be made overnight or after just one test.

You realize, too, that structuring experiences means Modeling. Find someone whose work is well respected, who consistently meets goals. Start with your upline. Observe them; get to know them. Find out what they do to be successful. What are their habits, techniques, routines? Then implement what you see and learn from them in your daily routine.

After you've taken "No" through the Five Step plan, notice that nothing has changed about "No." People still say "No," but it's just a word, not a threat to you. You've been diligent and patient, and you've allowed yourself to make mistakes along the way, with the end result that you have a whole new outlook on "No." Now you see "No" not only as a part of life, but also as a part of your business. You're able to hear "No" and continue building a relationship with that person. You're better at what you do because of "No." It elicits productive behavior from you, pushing you to talk to more people. "No" enhances your career.

A healthy feeling of self-esteem is the result, and your need is taken care of.

You put your belief through the Five Step plan, and it worked!

Deal with It

It would be helpful for all of us if we'd take the time to identify all of the stressors in our lives and then systematically put each of them through the Five Step plan. That would be one way we could understand which ones are posing as obstacles to us and why—and what we're going to do about them.

I know a man who is required to move regularly with his company. It's a good company, it has helped him progress quickly in his career, it more than meets the financial needs of his family, and the future looks bright.

This is a good job, and this man loves it dearly. He's not about to give it up. The line is deep and long waiting for jobs like his. He knows he's lucky to have it.

But he has a problem. Every time he has to move he thinks the world is coming to an end. He hates moving. He detests moving. Moving puts him in a foul mood. And yet, it's part of his job. He knows he will periodically be required to move to another part of the country.

I asked him once just why he hates moving so much, and he gave the rote answers. It's disruptive. The kids have to change schools. His wife has to make new friends. They have to sell the old house and buy a new one.

Moving is obviously a stressor for this man. Every three or four years, it causes him all sorts of unrest and pain.

I don't know him well enough to know exactly where his belief about "moving" was developed, but I know from his behavior that it's not, for him, an empowering belief. How do I know that? Well, first I know that it's his belief that drives his behavior, and I know by observing his behavior that it's producing results that don't meet his needs. Just the thought of moving can ruin his day. If his needs are not being met, that, by definition, means a hindering belief. An empowering one wouldn't have him in conflict. If he had an empowering belief on his Belief Lens, he wouldn't be in stress every time he moves.

If I were in his shoes, I'd want to change my belief about moving if I could. To do that, I'd employ the Five Step plan. First, I'd identify my stressor (moving) and the associated negative habitual emotional response (anxiety and anger).

Second, I'd ask "Why?" and "So what?" Through these questions I'd determine why I hated moving so much. Third, I'd get in touch with my life experiences that established my belief about moving—a belief that, through my behavior, says that moving is disruptive and painful. Maybe I'd find I had parents who moved a lot, and I had some bad experiences because of it; maybe that's where my pain comes from. Maybe I'd find I'd constantly heard others in the company complain about moving, and that left a major imprint on me.

Whatever I'd find, it would uncover why I had a hindering belief about moving.

Fourth, I'd identify a theoretical new belief about moving—something like: "Moving is good for my career. Because I am moving, I will continue to be successful and my family will prosper." In other words, moving is part of the path I choose to take, which will maximize my circumstances. Finally, for the fifth and final step, I'd structure Actual, Visualized, and Modeling experiences that would help me look at moving as a positive experience, not a negative one. Perhaps I'd arrange to coordinate a family vacation around the next move so it would be something to look forward to instead of more drudgery. I'd visualize the benefits I receive from my job that outweigh any negatives associated with moving. I'd look at the lives of people I want to emulate who used moving as an integral part of their success.

For Our Own Best Interest

Again, I wouldn't touch the stressor, I wouldn't change it one bit. The fact is, I couldn't change it. Moving would still entail all that it ever entailed. I wouldn't make a value judgment about moving for the whole world. But I most certainly would change my perception about moving. For me, it wouldn't be unpleasant any more. If I'm going to do it in my job and know I'm going to do it, and if the reasons I'm going to do it are in my best interest, then it's only for my own good that I establish a belief on my Belief Lens that says moving is good.

Only then will I drive behavior that produces results that meet my needs over time.

It's important to realize, too, that stressors are not universal. One person's stressor may be another person's motivator. One person may naturally crave having a deadline. It makes him or her work better while another person goes pale at the mere thought of a deadline. One person may covet speaking in front of a large group while the next person may fear that more than just about anything in the world.

Remember, stress is a response to a perception. If we perceive something as a threat, then it becomes our stressor. The less stressors, the better.

In business, stressors can occur on a companywide level or in a downline team as well. They need to be addressed just the same as individual stressors. The Five Step plan is just as applicable.

I knew an import company that for years had enjoyed a monopoly because no one else carried its main product. Then one year a rival company entered the arena. It, too, imported the same product. Suddenly, a race was on. Competition had entered the picture.

Most businesses aren't unduly unnerved by competition because it's part and parcel of their daily lives. But this particular company was unnerved. It wasn't used to the threats imposed by a competitor. Before this, its only worries had to do with customer service and market demand. Now it had to share the market.

Overnight and companywide, "competition" became a major stressor. Management began fearing for its existence. Employees began fearing for their jobs. The firm did not know how to respond to this new and menacing stressor. Competition frightened them. And it got worse before it got better. The company almost went out of business before it turned things around and became comfortable coexisting with the new rival on the block. The ironic twist was the competition ended up being a good thing. In the long term, both companies wound up selling well more than twice the amount of the original company when it operated strictly on its own.

Sadly, the original company had to undergo a couple of very stressful years until it was able to right itself.

Had it implemented the Five Step plan in the beginning, it could have dealt better with the new stressor on the block.

First, it would have identified the stressor as "competition."

Second, it would have asked, "Why?" and "So what?"

Third, it would have uncovered the hindering belief that was driving the neurotic, paranoid behavior causing the company to nearly go under—a belief that said, "Our value as a company is based on exclusivity of product."

Fourth, it would have replaced the hindering belief with a new empowering belief—one that said, "Our value as a company is based on our expertise to be able to sell whatever product we choose to distribute."

Finally, it would have structured experiences (Actual, Visualized, and Modeling), so people in all facets of the company would be able to successfully imprint the new empowering belief and obliterate the old hindering belief. They could have looked to and modeled other companies that succeeded because of competition.

Scrutiny, Scrutiny, Scrutiny

Whether it's personal or companywide, the questions we all want to keep asking ourselves are: "What beliefs are on my personal Belief Lens that are hindering me?" and "How can I change them to empowering beliefs?"

Since beliefs are sometimes well hidden, remember that the best way to get to the heart of our beliefs is through those things that squeak the loudest—namely, the stressors in our lives.

As we discussed earlier, a list of stressors could go on and on. We've listed just a few of them here. "Deadlines" and "moving" and "competition" are just the beginning of events that we might see as necessary stressors. We are all subject to them. If it's not traffic, it's expectations. If it's not worrying about relationships, it might be worrying about the behavior of our coworkers. It might be finances or emergencies. These stressors don't need to plague our lives, and they don't need to be altered as they're disempowered. That's the beauty of using principle-driven behavior to achieve our personal best. We don't need to change anything about the world. We don't have to eliminate anything. All we have to do is give up our old perception and replace it with a new one, based on an empowering belief. Just like that, what was once a stressor won't be a stressor anymore. Whatever it was will still be on our path, exactly as it was before, but we won't look at it with fear, trepidation, anxiety, and/or loathing anymore. We'll look at it as an asset. Our obstacles will turn into stepping-stones. Our deterrents will turn into encouragements.

Instant Replay

KEY POINTS

- The quality of our life is determined by the strength of our beliefs.

- There are five steps to reversing unproductive behaviors and responses:

  1. Identify situations that create negative emotional responses.

2.   Ask, "Why?" followed by, "So what? Why is that a threat?" to identify the belief and need.

3.   Identify the life experiences that created your belief.

4.   Identify a theoretical new belief or, "Why Not?"

5.   Structure experiences (Actual, Visualized, Modeling) to reinforce the new belief.

• Growth occurs when we apply the Five Step plan.

Personal Exercises

• Identify the recurring situations in your life (boss, deadlines, coworkers, finances) that cause negative emotional responses (frustration, anger, anxiety).

• Run these situations through the Five Step plan.

• Act on one structured experience every day for the next three weeks.

Where Do We Go from Here?

Now that we're plugged into recognizing empowering beliefs, in chapter fifteen we'll look at how to refine our focus to the point where we can recognize beliefs that are even more empowering.

CHAPTER FIFTEEN

A MORE EMPOWERING BELIEF

Refinement, refinement, refinement. Empowering beliefs can sometimes become even more empowering.

We've talked extensively about the need for changing hindering beliefs to empowering beliefs. It only makes sense to have beliefs in place that will drive behavior that will satisfy our needs.

Once an empowering belief is in place, what then?

Then the refinement process can begin.

If the definition of an empowering belief is one that meets my needs over time, then a belief that meets my needs even better over time is even more empowering.

Life is never stagnant, and the same holds true for beliefs. Let's say, by way of example, that you have a belief on your Belief Lens that says, "Daily exercise is important to me. It gives me the good health I need to be at my best in all my various roles." Now you've had that belief in place long enough to determine that it is an empowering belief for you. You know that because it drives behavior—an hour of exercise at least four days a week—that has produced results that over time have consistently helped you meet your needs. Because of that exercise, you enjoy general good health, your body feels fine, you're able to enjoy eating without constantly worrying about your waistline, and you have more energy for work, recreation, and family. Through exercise, you've helped satisfy your need to live, your self-esteem need, your need to enjoy, even your love need.

So you're not about to change your belief that drives your exercise behavior if you can help it. It works for you. It is empowering.

New Information

To continue our hypothetical example, let's say that you've noticed over the past few years that more and more of the people you exercise with are occasionally leaving the aerobic workout area—your usual domain—to move into the weight room and work out with weights. Your curiosity piqued, you ask your friends why they're working out with weights, and they tell you that exercise physiologists have conducted a number of tests over the past few years and have discovered many of the old myths about weight lifting being of little value from a health standpoint are just that— old myths. Their research suggests that the truth of the matter is that lifting weights can be very valuable from a health standpoint. The more all of our muscles are made to work, the more our body will respond with efficient function, and the more our metabolism will increase as a result. The best general exercise program couples aerobic exercise with some kind of weight work.

But your exercise consists exclusively of the aerobic variety. Your hour of exercising consists of running or bicycling or working out on aerobic machines in the gym. Every time you exercise, you faithfully get your heart rate up to an aerobic level and keep it there throughout your workout. You do all that because of a belief on your Belief Lens that says exercise is important to your health, and aerobic exercise is the best, most efficient form of exercise. Your heart gets a great workout, and afterward you feel great

Now that you've heard this new information, you're confronted with a decision: Do you alter your exercise routine so it includes both aerobic work and weight work? Or do you continue as you always have, because that's worked just fine for you?

New and Improved

You are faced with a more empowering belief than the one you've had in place. There wasn't anything wrong with your old belief. But now you've found a new and improved model.

Let's imagine that for years you'd walk past the weight room and dismiss weight lifting as something that was done primarily for vanity. You associated weight lifting with narcissistic behavior. Your perception was that bigger, stronger muscles didn't have much to do with good health. You never lifted weights.

Now you have new information. Now you have a decision to make. If your exercise behavior is going to include weight work, then first you're going to have to change what's on your Belief Lens about exercise with weights.

If you go ahead and change your belief from, "Daily aerobic exercise is important to my well-being" to "Daily aerobic exercise and weight work are important to my well-being," you've gone from a empowering belief to a more empowering belief.

At first you'll no doubt have a difficult time combining the two kinds of exercise. For one thing, your old perceptions about weight lifting will persist. Those imprints are the result of long-developed synapses. You may not make the change at all because of these difficulties. But if you choose to develop new imprints, you can. It's your choice. Gradually, the process will become easier and easier, and as a result, you will have satisfied your needs over time to an even healthier degree.

That's an easy example to see. While many of our beliefs may not be so easy to identify, the same rules apply. Just because a belief drives behavior that meets our needs doesn't mean that belief can't be refined and altered so it drives behavior that meets our needs even better!

Knowing Our Own Beliefs

It's a matter of getting to know what our beliefs are. When we do that, when we really get in touch with and understand our beliefs, then we put ourselves in a position to examine them carefully and see if they can become even more empowering.

I have seen this evolution from empowering to more empowering in action as I have worked with leaders in the Community Commerce industry. After one upline leader became familiar with the Belief Paradigm and the way the model helps illustrate the relationship between beliefs, behavior, and results, he decided to use the connection to help the distributors in his downline get in touch not only with the beliefs on their own personal Belief Lens, but also with the beliefs on the Belief Lens of their customers and prospects.

This upline leader had noticed a change over several years in the general public's perception of "network marketing." A combination of aggressive marketing efforts by other companies, who minimized the value of this leader's company's products and opportunities, and an increasing tendency by the media to portray network marketers in something less than a favorable light was creating problems in the industry. That was the trend, and it did not look healthy.

The leader saw a twofold danger inherent in this lowered perception of network marketers: One, the public would not just regard network marketers as having less value, but as less than honest. Two, members of his downline would think of their profession that way.

In other words, if either group—public or downline—bought into the belief that ,"network marketing is evil," well, there goes the neighborhood.

His desire was to stop any imprinting before it got out of hand. To that end, he brought all his downline members together and took them through the Belief Paradigm, just as we explained it in previous references. Then he asked each distributor to evaluate his or her own beliefs and behavior. Before looking at the beliefs that drive the behavior in their professional lives, he first asked them to look at the beliefs that drive the behavior in their personal lives. This upline was a good leader. He wanted them to buy the validity of the Belief Paradigm, and he knew that it would be easiest for them if they first saw the connection between beliefs, behavior, and results on a personal level.

Once they could individually relate to the Belief Paradigm, he moved into the area of professional beliefs and asked if there might be a chance that the negative campaigning currently so prevalent had diluted anyone's perception of their own profession. Had they bought into the belief that, "network marketing is evil?" Was that a belief that was driving their behavior in ways that were working against them? Perhaps an unconscious behavior, but a behavior just the same—and a negative one at that.

What was their behavior saying about the beliefs on their Belief Lens? That's what the upline leader wanted his downline to look at and consider.

If that behavior wasn't satisfying the necessary needs and, hence, reflected a hindering belief on the Belief Lens, he wanted his downline to accurately identify that hindering belief and change it to an empowering belief.

"With all the negative campaigning going on," the upline leader told me, "we recognized a danger that the typical network marketer's Belief Lens could reflect that negativity. They might not like themselves enough to be successful in selling or sharing the opportunity. If you're a distributor and you don't trust network marketing, and that's reflected by your behavior, then that's going to come right back to you. How can you say you don't trust network marketing and then say you trust yourself?"

The goal was to get at the root of the issue. Fix the problem, in other words, and not just the symptom. If a network marketer is only making ten calls a week instead of the group goal of say, fifty, don't look at the behavior (making only ten calls) but instead look at the belief that is driving that behavior. What's on the distributor's Belief Lens that's causing the reluctance to make more calls? Find the answer and change the belief, and the calls will shoot back up to fifty.

The upline leader also spoke with his downline members about the need to get in touch with what might be on the Belief Lens of their customers and prospects. If a customer or prospect has been drawn into the currently popular belief that "network marketing is evil," then that would explain the customer's behavior (i.e., declining interest, a lot of hesitation, unreturned phone calls).

Going to work to help the customer or prospect change that belief would be the necessary route to try to fix the problem. Polishing and re-polishing invitations and approaches, or continued emphasis on the product wouldn't change anything and would only cause the distributor to become more and more frustrated. Either change that belief or get a new client.

At the same time, however, the upline leader was careful to emphasize that it's important to always remember that it's only possible to have total control over your own area. He asked his downline to ask their customers questions such as: "What do you believe about us?" "What does our behavior tell you about us?" and "What can we do better to gain your complete trust?" These questions would allow the distributors to determine if there was anything they could do to help increase the customer's trust and improve their relationship.

"If the customer and the distributor are operating from the same set of beliefs, then there's going to be a sound foundation of trust," the upline leader said. "And that, in turn, will contribute to creating an atmosphere where the customer will take an objective look at the product, as well as the distributor, and not become sidetracked by anything else."

The upline leader's point is well taken. Looking at beliefs—that's what's important. For most of us, in all the areas of our lives, that means looking at our beliefs objectively and often. The world doesn't stand still, and the same applies to our beliefs. They should be constantly scrutinized and evaluated for optimum performance.

Results Tell the Tale

In the search for more empowering beliefs, it can sometimes be helpful to look at the end of the Belief Paradigm—the Results phase. That's the phase that tells us which of the four needs are best being met. It tells us if some might be better met than others and if there's a need for any adjustment.

Think of the four needs categories that we all have. Examine them one by one: the need to live, the love need, the self-esteem need, the need to enjoy. What beliefs are on our individual Belief Lens that are driving the behavior that's producing the results in each of these significant areas of needs? Could any of these beliefs, even if they are empowering, even if they're satisfying our needs, stand some upgrading? Some modernizing?

These are all good questions to ask. They are penetrating questions that can help us keep our beliefs in good running order. Again, the important point to remember is that there is no right or wrong when it comes to our beliefs, only empowering or hindering and, as we're now suggesting, more empowering.

The more empowering beliefs will drive behavior that will better meet our needs over time.

Looking at Other Beliefs

One of the best ways to search for more empowering beliefs is by looking at the behavior of others. Since behavior is the trail that leads to beliefs, when we see behavior that produces satisfying results in those around us, we have an opportunity to try to get in touch with the beliefs that drive that behavior.

George Plimpton, the noted "participatory author," wrote a book entitled *The X Factor* that I found to be a good example of "belief-probing." Plimpton's career as a journalist has been characterized by a penchant for firsthand experience. He once played a series of downs as quarterback for the Detroit Lions so he could write about what it felt like to actually play in a professional football game. For another story he put on the pads and the mask and played as a professional hockey goalie. On another occasion he got in the ring with a heavyweight boxing champion.

Through these experiences and others, George Plimpton became intrigued by an elusive, hard-to-define characteristic that seemed to be common to people the world sees as "winners."

Plimpton calls it the "X Factor." In his book he says it is common to those who greatly achieve, who "seem to be better than the sum of their parts."

What is the ingredient, he asks in the book's introduction:

> ...that appears to be a constant for those who are enormously successful. The "X Factor" I called it, though it is a quality which goes by many aliases: competitive spirit, the will to win, giving it 110 percent, the hidden spark, Celtic Green, Yankee pinstripes... guts, the killer instinct, *élan vital*, having the bit in one's teeth, and so on—qualities which if synthesized into liquid form and corked up in a bottle could be sold by the millions.

> The X Factor is obviously of extraordinary, even morbid, interest not only to sports journalists like myself, but to general managers, coaches, athletes, and indeed the general public.

> What is the ingredient that makes one athlete considerably better than another, though both are of equivalent physical skills? Even more mysterious, what is it that makes an entire team better than another when the general makeup of each is about the same?

In his quest, he interviewed and/or examined people in the world of business and in the world of sports, trying to determine what set them apart. They ranged from George Bush to Vince Lombardi; to former CEOs of the H. J. Heinz Company (Anthony O'Reilly) and IBM (Thomas J. Watson, Jr.); to Bill Russell, the great basketball star. He chose these individuals because of what they had accomplished—their results—and because of the behavior they exhibited in achieving those results.

He was hot on the trail of beliefs, in other words.

In the end, Plimpton doesn't quite get there. For his purposes, his search isn't specifically to define this elusive X Factor, but to paint a word picture of those who have it.

"One of the impulses in doing this sort of research," he writes, "was that some of the X Factor ingredients might rub off on me, as well as on the reader, and that a careful reading of the text and perhaps the practice of one or two of the exercises described could result in a mild transformation. I cannot promise as much, since it hasn't happened in my case. But one can hope for the best."

Go to the Source

The book is very entertaining, inspiring, and, as it applies to the power of personal truths, extremely intriguing because of what wasn't explored: the beliefs adhered to by these people who found success in so many different areas of life.

Find those out, and you've found the source.

For example, to understand what drove Vince Lombardi, the great football coach and winner of numerous championships, to say "Winning isn't everything, it's the only thing," it's essential to understand what beliefs were in place on his Belief Lens. Only by getting in touch with the very beliefs that drove his uncommon, tenacious behavior can we know why he behaved the way he did.

Indeed, the scrutiny of "great" men and women is a popular pastime for many. Biographies of people who have enjoyed great success and accomplishments are perennial best-sellers. Abraham Lincoln has been the subject of dozens of biographies and exhaustive historical probes. There is a seemingly insatiable desire to chart this great man's course, to relive his life, and perhaps to get some insight into why he was great.

Such study can be inspiring and educational. But where it can be most beneficial as it applies to our own lives is when we look beyond the behavior and look at the empowering beliefs that drove that behavior.

Lincoln's life provides a good illustration of this. It is easy to sit back and admire a man who saved the union and freed the slaves, accomplishments that preserve his place in history as America's greatest president.

It's when we examine his life more carefully, when we go beyond the results and try to determine the beliefs that drove him to act the way he acted, that we can appreciate what drove him so relentlessly to his triumphs.

According to the mountains of research into his life, Lincoln seemingly behaved according to one rock-solid belief that was immovable on his Belief Lens. He articulated that belief in his famous debates with Illinois senator Stephen A. Douglas when he said, "A house divided against itself cannot stand."

That was Lincoln's overriding belief. That was the belief that caused him to order the Union troops to stand their ground at Fort Sumter, precipitating the first armed engagement of the Civil War. Preserving the union was paramount to Lincoln. True to his strict Baptist roots, he didn't personally believe in slavery, but the moral question of slavery was not the primary issue that drove him as President of the United States. He believed, in fact, that the constitution protected slavery in the states where it already existed. But he also believed the constitution protected antislavery laws in states where they were implemented. As a result, slavery had become an issue that was dividing the union. As a president driven by a belief that the house could not be divided, Lincoln found that intolerable.

So he did everything he could to put the house back together. The end justified his means. After he became president in 1861, at a time when seven Southern states had already seceded from the union, he called every one of his chief presidential rivals to be members of his cabinet. The campaigning between these men had been bitter at times. These were men who didn't like Lincoln much and he didn't like them; but he saw the appointments of William H. Seward as secretary of state, Salmon P. Chase as secretary of the treasury, and Edward Bates as attorney general as essential if the union was to be preserved. So that's what he did. He sacrificed his personal feelings to stay true to his belief.

He went to extreme lengths in his efforts to preserve the union. He suspended various civil liberties from time to time during the war, including the writ of *habeas corpus*. Seizing on what he saw as a constitutional loophole, he delivered the Emancipation Proclamation in 1863, an act that freed the slaves, in the Confederacy because he interpreted that the constitution could only protect the rights to slavery in times of peace, not war.

In hindsight, it was clearly a stroke of genius. By the time the union had won the war, there was officially no slavery in the land. The house was no longer divided. Then the Thirteenth Amendment passed, which abolished slavery completely, ensuring that it could no longer pose a threat to divide the house.

At various junctures during this most perilous period in America's history, Lincoln's critics railed against his actions. He was called a dictator, a tyrant, an oppressor, a despot. But there was method to his madness. He was, in fact, none of these things. Over time his behavior reflected that, and he enjoyed favorable results. His beliefs empowered him and empowered the preserved union.

For a politician to look at the life of, say, Abraham Lincoln and benefit from his successes would be a most productive exercise. Just as it would be productive for a salesman to look at beliefs that have worked for great salesmen, or for an athlete to look at beliefs that have worked for great athletes, or for an artist to look at beliefs that have worked for great artists.

We're in Control

In the final analysis, the point is that it's important to realize that we're in control of our beliefs, and not vice versa. They can be altered, adjusted, amended, revised. They can be changed when it makes sense to change them, when it means behavior that will better produce results that meet our needs over time.

When an empowering belief meets a more empowering belief, it only makes sense to adjust and adopt the belief that is more empowering.

There is a classic story I'd like to relate that sums up what I'm trying to say. It involves a navy captain aboard a battleship. The battleship is underway in the ocean, going full steam. It's night, and all the ship's lights are on, when the captain sees, off in the distance on the horizon, another light.

He gets on the radio.

"Attention," he calls out. "We are on a collision course. Change your course 30 degrees."

"I suggest that you change your course 30 degrees instead," comes the reply.

"I'm a captain, and I'm ordering you to change your course," indignantly responds the captain.

"I'm a seaman first class and I still suggest that you change your course," comes the reply.

By now incensed by this insolence, the captain plays his hole card and responds authoritatively, "We are a battleship."

To which the seaman replies, "We are a lighthouse."

An empowering belief was about to meet a more empowering belief, and the captain adjusted accordingly.

Instant Replay

Key Points

- We can have personal breakthroughs by replacing empowering beliefs with more empowering beliefs.

- Studying the lives of successful people helps us identify the more empowering beliefs we can apply in our lives.

Personal Exercises

- Identify areas of your life that you would like to take to a higher level.

- Model your life after someone who is already at a higher level to identify a more empowering belief and how to implement it.

Where Do We Go from Here?

In chapter sixteen, I'd like to share a number of success stories. I've seen this "power" drive meaningful growth in many lives, particularly my own.

CHAPTER SIXTEEN

CHANGE HAPPENS

It really does! My life changed through the power of beliefs, and I've seen countless others reflect this change in their lives as well.

Whenever I'm asked what it is that drives my fervor for the meaningful changes that can come into our lives through adopting new beliefs, my answer is always the same: My enthusiasm comes from personal experience. I have seen meaningful change happen in my own life, and I have seen it happen in the lives of many others. I have seen it work! Seeing lives change for the better through the application of empowering individual beliefs is a thrilling experience and one that never gets old. For that reason, my enthusiasm has only increased over the years.

Changes Everywhere

The changes I have seen come in all areas and walks of life. Often, even though the original emphasis is on job satisfaction and performance, the changes that take place are far afield from the workplace. There was the case of one employee in a company in the Midwest who, after learning about the Belief Paradigm and the benefits that result when empowering beliefs drive behavior, took his newfound tools to the aid of his teenage son, an eighth-grader who was having difficulties in the classroom. It seemed that very early in his schooling, the son had been tagged by child psychologists as a "slow learner." Although there was no hard evidence to support the slow-learner theory, the news nonetheless got through loud and clear to the son, who dutifully imprinted that message and labeled himself as a "slow learner." Consequently, his grades and classroom performance in general were quite poor and showed no sign of changing.

The boy's father decided to use the Belief Paradigm as a vehicle to help his son understand what was driving his poor classroom behavior. He and his wife sat down with their son and patiently drew out the Belief Paradigm, starting with the Needs Quadrants and continuing through the Belief Lens, the Behavior, the Results, and the timeline connecting Results back to the Needs Quadrants. They explained to their son how our behavior is the direct result of the beliefs we've put on our Belief Lens, and how the results of our behavior reflect those beliefs. They further explained how important it is to analyze the results of our behavior in connection with our needs. If our needs are being met, then the results are a product of behavior being driven by beliefs that empower us. If our needs are not being met, on the other hand, then the results are a product of behavior being driven by beliefs that hinder us.

For the first time, by utilizing the Belief Paradigm, both the parents and the teenage son looked realistically at what was driving the behavior of this eighth-grade student. They realized he had a belief that said he couldn't do well in school because he was a "slow learner." As long as he kept that belief, it would stay on his Belief Lens, and his behavior would translate into results that would reinforce the image he had of himself as a "slow learner." The problem was his self-esteem need was taking a beating as a result. And his grades weren't looking too good, either.

If new imprinting could take place and create a new belief that said, "I am not a slow learner. If I study, concentrate, and work hard I can be successful in the classroom," the results could reflect a completely different kind of behavior and, when analyzed, could show success at meeting the teenager's self-esteem necessity.

A Successful Change of Belief

Such imprinting did take place. The family, in effect, went through the Five Step plan. They identified the stressor and asked, "Why?" and "So what?" They identified where the hindering belief came from, came up with a theoretical new belief, and structured experiences to imprint that new principle. As a result, a "good learner" was born out of what had been labeled a "slow learner."

That father's experience served to reinforce something that had been impressed upon me over and over again during my competitive athletic career: People categorize themselves and then stay in that category by habit. Race after race and year after year I noticed this phenomenon. As I've discussed earlier, more often than not, runners would finish where they thought they should finish. I remember how much this worked to my advantage—quite inadvertently I might add—when I was trying to make my fourth United States Olympic team at the Olympic Track and Field Trials in the summer of 1988.

I had come down with a case of pneumonia prior to the meet and was barely getting better by the time of my semifinal race. I needed to place in the top six to be able to move on to the finals—no small task, I knew, under the circumstances.

Trying to conserve my energy, I ran as easily as I could with an eye not on winning the semifinal but on making it into the top six. All was going well enough until the final lap when a runner passing me on the inside while jumping over a barrier cut too close and knocked me down. As I fell to the track, I stuck my hand out to cushion the blow and the runner in front of me accidentally caught my hand with the spikes on the bottom of his shoe. I was bleeding and flat out on the track—and by now a good twenty yards behind the field—with only 200 yards to the finish line.

That's when my expectations took over and, I have to believe, when the expectations of those I was running against also took over. I was an eight-time national champion. I knew it. They knew it. I thought I'd place in the top six. They thought I'd place in the top six. I got to my feet and did what we all thought I'd do. I made up those twenty yards, passing just enough runners to finish, you guessed it, in sixth place. In the finals two days later, with the cut in my hand stitched, I was able to qualify for the Seoul Olympics.

There is another example of two mid-level executives who made what some would consider rather drastic changes while being trained in this material. Their company was going through a reengineering overhaul, and, as you might imagine, there was a lot of soul-searching going on as to the changes inherent with that reengineering. Both executives were faced with, "Is this what I want to do with my life?" questions.

Different Answers

They wound up answering them in different ways. One decided to switch to part-time status with the company and the other decided to leave entirely. Neither decision was based on dissatisfaction with the new direction the company was heading, however. Instead, each decision was based on values and needs. Both of these executives took a good, honest look at what they wanted most in life and acted upon what they saw.

The executive who switched to part-time status did so because he realized he wanted to devote more time to his wife and family—areas he felt he had neglected for too long. He turned down an opportunity to become a chief player in the company's reengineering because along with the promotion would come longer working hours and an increased workload. He was in a position where he could still provide for his family financially, while at the same time cutting back on his company involvement. Because his value system placed a premium on his family relationships, and because he sensed a need to place more of an emphasis in terms of time and energy in that area, he made a meaningful change in his life that would better satisfy his necessities.

The executive who left the company entirely also turned down what would have been a promotion in the reengineering process. He elected instead to pursue a goal he'd had in the back of his mind for several years: playing on the professional Senior Golf Tour. He assessed his situation and decided he was financially well equipped to be able to take two years off for intensive practice, after which he'd go out and give the tour a shot. There was no guarantee that he'd be successful as a professional golfer, but he had the full-fledged support and encouragement of his spouse and family, who all agreed that the satisfaction was going to be in the trying. He didn't have to make it; all he had to do was give it his best and enjoy the process. With all that support behind his pursuit, he turned in his notice at work and then went to work on his short game.

In this example, neither executive had a problem with his job. Both had performed long enough and well enough that they were in a position for excellent promotions. They each also realized upon reflection that there were other values in their lives that also had meaning. By putting the right beliefs in place, change wasn't difficult. Quite the opposite was true. Change was welcomed.

Give It Time

Helping people get in touch with those meaningful values is what's at the heart of my work. I often ask people to incorporate into their lives their chosen "new" beliefs for twenty-one days—enough time to formulate new habits—after they have been introduced to the Belief Paradigm and the concept of achieving one's personal best by implementing empowering beliefs. Over the years, I have heard numerous stories of how, in the course of twenty-one days, lives have been changed.

Those twenty-one-day experiences provide a constant stream of positive reinforcement that behavior based on empowering beliefs indeed changes people's lives and helps them achieve new personal bests. The most gratifying part of my profession is seeing people lead happier, healthier, and more productive lives as a result of applying these concepts in their lives.

Let's look at another example to further illustrate. This story comes from a company on the West Coast and involves a woman in her early forties who had been a legal secretary most of her working life. She had an affinity for the law and was in high demand as a secretary, often doing the same research and document preparation as the lawyers she worked for.

For years this secretary had squelched a desire to become an attorney because of all the reasons you might imagine. She was too old, she had a family to care for—those were two of the reasons. And of course there was the big one—that she was a woman!

That last reason she didn't precisely articulate to herself. It was an imprint, an unconscious yet very powerful belief. She had grown up in a home with an authoritative father who, while kind and gentle in most ways, was very much a male chauvinist. He was a banker, and at his bank all the managers were men and all the tellers, as well as the secretaries, were women. He did not encourage his daughter to go to college, although her brothers were encouraged to get their degrees. He did not encourage his daughter to forge a professional career. He encouraged her to be a homemaker, like her mother, or, at the very most, a secretary. This woman had been raised by a staunch traditionalist.

So that was her imprint, and it created a strong belief that said, "Women are subservient to men." She carried that belief onto her Belief Lens, which drove her behavior to become a secretary and to remain a secretary.

This woman wasn't driven to change by participating in my seminar, however. Her process of changing beliefs was much like mine when I left the law—she did it on her own. When the pain got great enough for her, she did something about it. Her pain came in the form of seeing lawyers make considerably more money than she did every payday, even though they performed many of the same tasks and worked the same number of hours. Comparing a $15-an-hour secretary's pay to a $125-an-hour lawyer's pay is painful in its own way. Her pain also came in the dull ache she constantly felt in knowing she was stifling her potential.

So she went to law school. She was the oldest person in her class. And the smartest. She sacrificed some things in her life during her three years of law school and put other things on hold, but when the three years were up—and the time went faster than she imagined it would—she had her diploma. She was a card-carrying member of the bar. The firm that valued her services so much as a secretary hired her first as a clerk, then as an associate, and, before long, she became a partner in the firm. The new belief on her Belief Lens—"Women can perform tasks equally as well as men"—had driven her to a change that was very significant and meaningful in her life.

Change Doesn't Have to Be Extreme

Such success stories are heartwarming and serve as excellent examples for others to follow. I always like to throw out a caution, however, that examples of extreme career changes shouldn't mislead us into thinking that change has to mean drastic and dramatic leaps.

Many times a realistic look at our beliefs allows us to be content with our current circumstances. Or it might prod us to effect change that is less dramatic than a wholesale change of career or environment. Subtle change is effective, too. Sometimes it's the minor adjustments that make all the difference.

For instance, working at what might be considered an entry-level job can nonetheless be quite fulfilling and satisfying for the person who has a large family to care for and recognizes the value of having the employment. If our empowering beliefs are in place, paying dues becomes much easier to do. We're willing to be patient and put up with more because of the knowledge we have inside that our needs will be best met over time.

Besides generating meaningful change, a clear understanding of the power of our beliefs also helps make us aware of the physiological occurrences that take place in our lives as we deal with the various mental obstacles and threats that constantly appear. When we realize that our bodies generate toxins, for example, after cortisol is released during vigilant responses, we also realize we must disperse those toxins through physical exertion. Many trainers I've worked with have had experiences with people who credit this awareness with literally saving their lives.

When we know what's going on, in other words, we then put ourselves in a position to do something about it. All of the preventive medicine measures, such as exercise, financial planning, time management, and relationship skills, take on more real significance. All of a sudden, "going to the gym," has more incentive behind it than simply, "I gotta work on the old waistline." All of a sudden, sitting down and working out a financial budget that concentrates on spending less than you make is a worthwhile exercise. All of a sudden, planning a trip to Yosemite with your spouse, "just to see the falls we've always wanted to see," makes perfect sense. All of a sudden, making time for a trek in the Himalayas isn't so selfish and self-centered after all.

That's because we are in touch with our beliefs, which means we're in touch with ourselves, and the tremendous part about that is we finally have total control of ourselves.

The Concept of "Over Time"

Empowering beliefs give us the energy, the stamina, the enthusiasm, to go on with what's important to us in our lives, to keep striving. Empowering beliefs give us the concept of "over time." Empowering beliefs enable us to quit sacrificing what we want most for what we want now.

Without an empowering belief on my personal Belief Lens, I am convinced I would have quit track and field after the 1984 Olympic Games. When the Olympic medal I had been pursuing most of my life landed just out of my grasp, I truly believe I would have packed it in then and there if my behavior had still been driven by the belief that my success and self-worth were dependent upon beating other people and winning medals.

Luckily, my personal finish line was internal, and I was able to absorb the disappointment as a personal triumph. I felt good about giving that Olympic race everything I had. I felt a sense of personal peace and calm.

That peace and calm not only enabled me to continue on as a competitor, but to thrive. By the time the 1985 season began and the virus had mercifully run its course—although it would persist throughout the rest of my career—I was ready to go. I participated in the usual early season meets, finding my competitive legs once again. By the time the national championships came along, I was in good enough shape to capture my eighth straight national steeplechase title. By the fall of that season, after months of serious training, I was able to achieve what for me were two significant personal goals. The first came in Bern, Switzerland, when I ran a sub-four-minute mile for the first time in my life. I know, I was a steeplechaser, and steeplechasers aren't milers, but since my goals were set inwardly, that accomplishment meant a great deal to me even if the world took absolutely no notice. My achievement of that "milestone" of breaking the four-minute barrier was personally very gratifying.

The second significant goal was realized in August of 1985 in Koblenz, Germany. I was determined to not only lower my own American steeplechase record that night on the track, but break the 8:10 barrier as well—a barrier that, to that point in time, had been broken by only four other runners.

As I previously related, I visualized that night's race all during the afternoon, programming in my mind the exact pace I needed to run. The existing American record, as well as my personal best time, was an 8:12.37 I had run in 1983, so I knew I had my work cut out for me. Two and a half seconds is a relative eternity in a 3,000-meter race. But I was determined, and in my own mind I felt I was ready. Since the Olympic "disappointment" a year ago, I had trained better than anytime in my life.

The race went like (pardon the expression) clockwork. I hit every split right on and then, on the gun lap, found a little extra. I'd found that two and a half seconds and a little to spare. I finished in 8:09.17. I placed first in eleven of the twelve races I entered in 1985. In the twelfth race, which took place in Australia, I got out leaned at the tape after having just made a trip from European competitions. It was the best year I'd ever enjoyed during my steeplechasing career, and it came after what most people saw as my biggest disappointment.

I know I couldn't have kept running at such a high level if every time I walked onto a track I dwelt on how unfair life had been to me at the Olympic Games of 1984, and that I was somehow a failure because I had been beaten by other people.

My principle of not quitting until I'd given my best drove me to a long and satisfying running career—one that included a top ten world ranking for twelve straight years and the second highest number of ranking points ever accumulated by a steeplechaser (one point behind Bronislaw Malinowski of Poland, the gold-medal winner of the 1980 Moscow Olympic Games). I started to gradually slow down after 1985 but, still, there was another Olympic Games on the horizon in Seoul, South Korea, in 1988, and I determined that I wanted to make that my curtain call. I trained accordingly and at the age of thirty-four wound up placing sixth in an Olympic final that turned out to be the fastest steeplechase race ever. I remember the emotion I felt when that race was over. I was satisfied I had done what I'd promised myself that day many years ago in Provo, Utah, when I returned to the BYU track long enough "to see how far I could go, to see just what I could do." Before I left the Olympic stadium, I knelt down and kissed the track good-bye. Most of the 80,000 people in the stands either took no notice or wondered what on earth that American who finished sixth was doing kissing the track. I wasn't the winner in their minds. But, thankfully, I was in mine.

INDEX

A

Actual Experiences: 184, 188, 189
Addictions: 91, 92, 94, 100, 104
Adrenaline: 75, 79
Advertising: 37, 38
Aerobic exercise: 109
Affirmations: 116
Ali, Muhammad: 60, 61
Arby's: 41, 42
Assets: 144
Athletics West: 199
Avoidance: 92

B

Bates, Edward: 233
Bell, Gerald: 2
Blackwood, James: 33, 194
Blame: 25
Bowerman, Bill: 194
Boys Town: 21, 22
Budd, Zola: 200, 204
Bush, George: 231

C

Carter, Jimmy: 195
Caterpillar company: 183
Change: vii, 106, 128, 178, 179, 234, 237, 239, 241, 243
Chase, Salmon P.: 233
Choice: 69
Civil War: 58, 59, 60, 232
Consequences: 15
Contraction band lesions: 81
Control: xix, 70, 135, 137, 139, 142, 215, 234
Corpus Christi King High School: 33
Cortisol: 77
Cousins, Norman: 118
Creativity: 118

D

Dallas Cowboys: 31
Darrow, Clarence: 63
Decker-Slaney, Mary: 199, 203, 204
Depression: 129

Depression, Great: 129
Detroit Lions: 230
Diemer, Brian: 198, 201
Douglas, Stephen A.: 232

E

Emancipation Proclamation: 233
Exercise: 45, 55, 68, 86, 100,
    103, 107, 109, 111, 121,
    133, 147, 162, 172, 173,
    176, 190, 205
Expression: 118

F

Finances: 112
Fitness: 105
Five Step plan: 209, 210, 211,
    213, 216, 217, 218, 219,
    220, 222, 239
Flanagan, Edward Joseph: 21
Flannery, Raymond: 139
Flowing: 141, 142
Football: 31, 33
Foreman, George: 60, 61
Franklin, Benjamin: xix, 70, 100
Frankl, Viktor: 187
Frazier, Joe: 60
Freedom: xviii, 9

G

Golden Rule: 16
Golf: 126, 241

H

Habits: 178
Harding, Wendell: 32
Harvard Medical School: 139
Haynes, Racehorse: 63
Hemingway, Ernest: 89

Hitler, Adolf: xiii
Hockey: vii
Hogan, Ben: 125
Holocaust: 100, 142
Holzworth, Sheila: 43
Homeostasis: 13

I

Iacocca, Lee: 128
IBM: 231
Imprinting: 35, 38, 45

J

James, Sherald: 48, 194
Jenner, Bruce: 193
Jones, Bobby: 125

K

Kamikaze Corps: 30
Kariuki, Julius: 200
Korir, Julius: 200

L

Lewis, Carl: 200
Lincoln, Abraham: 232, 234
Lindbergh, Charles: 99, 124, 126
Lombardi, Vince: 231
Love need: 18

M

Mahmoud, Joseph: 201
Malinowski, Bronislaw: 246
Malone, Karl: 99
Maminski, Boguslaw: 195
Marriott Corporation: 130, 131
metabolic rate: 109, 110, 111,
    112
Modeling: 183, 189, 190, 210,
    216, 218, 220, 222

About the Author

Henry Marsh became the second American male runner to make four U.S. Olympic track teams in 1988. His career culminated with thirteen straight years as one of the top ten 3,000-meter steeplechase runners in the world—three years as number one. He has also held the American record for an unprecedented twenty-six years in a row and still holds the second fastest time every by an American. During that time, Henry graduated cum laude in economics from BYU and received his law degree from the University of Oregon.

After practicing law with the Salt Lake City firm of Parsons, Behle & Latimer, Henry became a consultant for the Franklin Covey Company before moving on to become one of the founders of MonaVie, an international health and wellness company. In these roles he has worked to help people achieve their dreams and change their futures through adopting principle-driven behaviors.

Henry resides in Utah with his family, but continues to travel and present to audiences around the world.